Circular Blue Economy: Advancing Climate Change Action with Blue Economy Innovation, Marine Conservation, Sustainability, Renewable Energy, and Ocean Resources

I0022938

Copyright

Circular Blue Economy: Advancing Climate Change Action with Blue Economy Innovation, Marine Conservation, Sustainability, Renewable Energy, and Ocean Resources

ISBN (eBook): 978-1-991368-53-9

ISBN (Paperback): 978-1-991368-54-6

Published by Global Climate Solutions

First Edition, 2025

Cover design and interior layout by Global Climate Solutions

Table of Contents

Introduction

The circular blue economy represents a shift in how societies manage and benefit from ocean and coastal resources. It moves beyond traditional linear models of extraction, use, and disposal toward approaches that prioritize regeneration, efficiency, and long-term sustainability. This framework recognizes the interconnected nature of marine ecosystems, economic activities, and community well-being, and emphasizes the need to maintain the health of the ocean as a foundation for economic prosperity and social stability. By integrating circular economy principles into blue economy sectors, countries and communities can reduce waste, optimize resource use, and support the restoration of marine environments.

The concept builds on the understanding that oceans provide essential services that sustain life and livelihoods, including climate regulation, biodiversity support, food production, and economic opportunities. However, increasing pressures from overexploitation, pollution, habitat loss, and climate change place these systems at risk. Circularity offers tools and strategies to address these challenges by designing production and consumption processes that minimize environmental impacts and promote regenerative outcomes. This includes creating closed-loop systems, adopting sustainable materials, and incorporating nature-based solutions into development plans.

Innovation plays a central role in advancing the circular blue economy. New technologies such as digital monitoring systems, bio-based materials, and renewable energy solutions support more efficient and environmentally responsible practices. Digitalization enhances transparency and accountability across marine supply chains, enabling better tracking of resources, compliance with regulations, and optimization of operations. Advances in marine biotechnology contribute to developing sustainable products derived from marine organisms, while renewable energy systems such as offshore wind and tidal power support decarbonization efforts. These innovations help reduce the environmental footprint of marine industries and create opportunities for sustainable economic growth.

Governance frameworks guide the implementation of circular strategies by establishing rules, incentives, and collaborative mechanisms. International agreements, regional initiatives, and national policies define responsibilities and promote coordinated action. Marine spatial planning, waste management regulations, and conservation policies help ensure that development aligns with ecological limits and social priorities. Effective governance involves inclusive processes that incorporate the perspectives of coastal communities, Indigenous peoples, private sector actors, and civil society organizations. This inclusivity strengthens legitimacy, improves compliance, and supports outcomes that benefit a wider range of stakeholders.

Communities are central to the success of circular blue economy transitions. Coastal populations rely on marine resources for food, culture, and livelihoods, and many have developed practices that emphasize stewardship and long-term sustainability. Community-driven initiatives, such as local fisheries management, seaweed cultivation, and coastal restoration, demonstrate how circular principles can be embedded into daily practices. Empowering communities through education, capacity building, and equitable access to resources enhances their ability to participate in decision-making and benefit from new opportunities.

Finance and investment influence the pace and scale of circular transformation. Sustainable finance instruments, including blue bonds and blended finance models, direct capital toward activities that support environmental regeneration and sustainable economic development. Investment frameworks that incorporate environmental, social, and governance criteria help ensure that financial flows contribute to resilience and long-term value. By shifting investment priorities, public and private actors can accelerate the adoption of circular practices across marine sectors.

The circular blue economy provides a path toward protecting marine ecosystems while supporting sustainable development. It encourages integrated approaches that consider ecological, economic, and social dimensions, helping countries address climate change, biodiversity loss, and resource depletion. As global interest in sustainable ocean management grows, circularity offers a coherent framework for aligning policies, practices, and investments with the goal of maintaining healthy oceans and resilient coastal communities.

Chapter 1: Foundations of the Circular Blue Economy

This chapter introduces the underlying concepts that shape the circular blue economy, exploring the evolution of blue economy thinking and its intersection with circularity. It examines the principles that guide regenerative and resource-efficient approaches in marine contexts. The chapter outlines how traditional ocean-based industries can transition toward systems that minimize waste, restore ecosystems, and support long-term sustainability.

Origins and Evolution of Blue Economy and Circular Economy Concepts

The Blue Economy emerged as a framework for managing ocean and coastal resources in ways that support economic development while maintaining ecological health. It gained prominence in the early 2010s as nations recognized the growing importance of marine sectors such as fisheries, aquaculture, tourism, shipping, and offshore energy. Early definitions emphasized sustainable use of marine resources and highlighted the need to balance growth with conservation. Over time, the concept expanded to include a wider set of ecological considerations, reflecting concerns about declining fish stocks, marine pollution, and the impacts of climate change on oceans. International organizations, governments, and research institutions played a central role in promoting the Blue Economy as an approach that integrates economic opportunity with environmental responsibility.

Parallel to this, the Circular Economy developed as a response to the limitations of linear production systems that relied on extraction, manufacturing, consumption, and disposal. Pioneered by ecological economists and industrial ecology researchers, the Circular Economy emphasized closed-loop systems in which materials and resources circulate through reuse, recycling, and regeneration. The approach challenged the traditional model by proposing that waste should be designed out of production systems altogether. Influential reports, particularly those produced by research foundations and global industry platforms, helped build momentum by demonstrating how circular principles could reduce environmental impacts while supporting innovation and economic efficiency. Governments and businesses began adopting circular strategies across sectors ranging from manufacturing to waste management, recognizing the opportunity to reduce resource dependency and improve sustainability.

As global resource pressures intensified, the two frameworks started to intersect more clearly. Marine industries faced rising levels of pollution, habitat degradation, and overexploitation, prompting the search for more resilient economic models. The concept of the Circular Blue Economy emerged as a way to integrate circular principles directly into the marine context. It applied ideas such as product life extension, resource recovery, and regenerative design to ocean-based industries. For example, in fisheries and aquaculture, circularity encouraged better use of byproducts and organic waste, as well as system designs that reduce environmental impacts. In coastal infrastructure, circular principles influenced materials choices, design for disassembly, and approaches to managing end-of-life components. In tourism and shipping, circularity promoted improved resource efficiency and waste reduction practices.

Global policy processes contributed to the evolution of these ideas. Major environmental agreements highlighted the need to tackle marine pollution, protect ecosystems, and improve resource efficiency. This created an enabling environment for integrating circular principles into marine strategies. National blue economy plans in several countries began referencing resource recovery, sustainable design, and waste minimization alongside traditional growth objectives. The European Union, for instance, incorporated circularity into its ocean strategies and action plans, linking marine policy with broader circular economy initiatives. Regional seas conventions and international bodies also began addressing issues such as marine litter, port waste reception, and sustainable fisheries through circular frameworks.

Simultaneously, advances in technology supported the transition toward more circular approaches. Digital tools made it possible to track resources, monitor marine environments, and improve transparency across supply chains. Emerging materials science enabled the development of bio-based and recyclable materials suited to marine conditions. Innovations in renewable energy technologies expanded the potential for cleaner production and reduced reliance on fossil fuels in maritime operations. These developments strengthened the link between circular practices and blue economy objectives by improving both environmental performance and long-term economic viability.

The evolution of the Circular Blue Economy reflects a convergence of environmental awareness, technological progress, and policy commitment. As understanding of ocean systems has grown, so too has recognition that economic activity must align with ecological resilience and resource efficiency. The merging of blue and circular principles represents an effort to create economic models that work with natural systems rather than against them, using design and innovation to reduce impacts and enhance long-term sustainability across marine industries.

Principles of Circularity: Reduce, Reuse, Recycle, Regenerate

Circularity in marine and coastal systems is grounded in a set of principles designed to minimize resource inputs, limit waste generation, and maintain ecological functions. These principles guide the transition from linear models toward systems that keep materials circulating for longer periods and rely on natural processes to restore ecosystems. In the context of the Blue Economy, applying these principles requires changes in how products are designed, how industries operate, and how marine resources are managed across their full life cycle.

The principle of reduce focuses on minimizing the use of materials, energy, and water throughout production and consumption processes. In marine sectors, reduction strategies aim to decrease pressure on natural resources and limit emissions, discharges, and waste. This includes improving the efficiency of fishing operations, optimizing feed and nutrient inputs in aquaculture, and lowering energy use in shipping and port activities. Designers and manufacturers consider material intensity and durability when developing products for marine use, such as equipment for offshore energy systems or coastal infrastructure components. Reduction also involves preventing unnecessary extraction of marine resources by improving monitoring, adopting more accurate forecasting tools, and adjusting harvesting practices based on ecosystem conditions. Reducing overall demand for raw materials lowers the environmental footprint of marine industries and supports more sustainable resource flows.

Reuse focuses on extending the lifespan of materials and products through repair, refurbishment, or direct second-life applications. In the marine environment, reuse strategies are increasingly relevant for gear, vessels, infrastructure components, and equipment used in offshore industries. For example, fishing nets and ropes can be designed for multiple lifecycles or repurposed into new applications when they are no longer suitable for their original use. Maritime equipment, including navigation aids, buoys, and port machinery, may be restored or adapted rather than replaced. Reuse practices reduce the need for new materials, lower operational costs, and decrease the volume of waste entering the ocean. In many cases, digital tools and remote monitoring systems support reuse by allowing operators to track equipment performance, schedule maintenance efficiently, and identify components that can be recovered or redeployed.

Recycle involves transforming materials at the end of their useful life into new products or raw materials. Recycling efforts in marine sectors address a range of materials, including plastics from coastal communities, waste generated in ports, and end-of-life components from aquaculture and offshore energy installations. Effective recycling requires systems for collection, sorting, and processing, as well as markets for the recovered materials. Ports and coastal municipalities play a role by providing facilities that support waste segregation and recycling. Industries are increasingly exploring the use of recycled content in new products, reducing dependency on virgin materials and lowering environmental impacts associated with extraction and manufacturing. Advances in materials science support higher-quality recycling processes, including chemical recycling techniques that break down plastics into base components suitable for reuse in multiple marine applications.

Regenerate refers to restoring natural ecosystems and enhancing their capacity to provide environmental services. This principle recognizes that healthy marine ecosystems support fisheries, protect coastlines, store carbon, and sustain biodiversity. Regeneration efforts include restoring seagrass meadows, mangrove forests, coral reefs, and other coastal habitats that have been degraded by pollution, overuse, or climate-related impacts. In fisheries and aquaculture, regenerative practices involve maintaining nutrient cycles, protecting breeding grounds, and implementing ecosystem-based management approaches. Industries that operate in marine environments can contribute to regeneration by minimizing seabed disturbance, restoring habitats affected by infrastructure development, and adopting nature-based solutions that enhance ecological functions. Regeneration is also linked to cultural and community practices that prioritize stewardship of marine ecosystems and promote sustainable interaction with coastal environments.

Applying these principles in combination creates synergies across marine sectors. Reduction strategies lower demand for new materials and prevent unnecessary extraction. Reuse and recycling keep materials circulating, decreasing waste flows and reducing the volume of debris entering the ocean. Regenerative practices rebuild the natural systems that support life and economic activity along coasts and in open waters. Together, these principles form the foundation of circularity in the Blue Economy and inform the design of policies, technologies, and business models that operate within ecological limits.

Distinctions and Intersections with Traditional Blue Economy Frameworks

Traditional Blue Economy frameworks focus on harnessing marine and coastal resources to drive economic development while maintaining ecological sustainability. These frameworks emphasize sectoral growth in areas such as fisheries, aquaculture, tourism, shipping, and offshore energy. The central aim is to balance economic opportunity with conservation by promoting responsible practices, improving management systems, and encouraging investment in sustainable marine industries. While this approach advances environmental considerations, it generally operates within existing production and consumption models that prioritize resource extraction and efficiency rather than systemic transformation.

Circularity introduces a broader perspective by addressing the full life cycle of materials, products, and infrastructure. Rather than focusing primarily on managing impacts, circular approaches aim to eliminate waste, reduce resource use, and design systems that regenerate natural environments. This shift encourages industries to rethink how resources are used at every stage, from production to end-of-life. In the marine context, it involves redesigning fishing gear to prevent loss, creating closed-loop aquaculture systems, and ensuring materials used in offshore structures can be reused or recycled. Circularity also stresses the importance of restoring ecosystems that support economic activity, expanding the scope beyond conservation toward regeneration.

A key distinction lies in how the two frameworks conceptualize resource flows. Traditional Blue Economy strategies seek to optimize resource use within a largely linear model of extraction, production, and disposal. Efficiency gains are encouraged, but the underlying system remains dependent on a continuous flow of raw materials. Circular models, by contrast, aim to slow, narrow, or close resource loops. They propose reducing inputs, reusing products, and recovering materials that would otherwise become waste. This creates opportunities for new business models, such as product-as-a-service systems in maritime industries or resource-recovery ventures linked to coastal waste streams.

Governance approaches also differ. Traditional Blue Economy policies typically focus on managing individual sectors through regulatory frameworks, licensing systems, spatial planning, and conservation measures. These tools address specific impacts but may not fully integrate cross-sector linkages. The Circular Blue Economy introduces a more systemic orientation, encouraging policies that link waste management, energy systems, materials use, and ecosystem restoration. This includes extended producer responsibility schemes, circular design standards for maritime infrastructure, and investment frameworks that support resource-efficient technologies. The intersection with national circular economy strategies becomes more pronounced as governments align marine policies with broader sustainability and climate goals.

Technological integration represents another point of divergence. Traditional frameworks emphasize technologies that improve efficiency, such as precision fishing tools, sustainable aquaculture practices, or cleaner maritime fuels. Circular approaches incorporate these innovations while also supporting systems that track materials, optimize reuse, and enable recycling. Digital tools such as blockchain can provide traceability for seafood supply chains, while sensors and monitoring systems help identify lost gear that can be recovered and repurposed. Technologies that improve waste collection and processing in ports further support circular practices, linking marine industries with circular value chains.

Economic models show both distinctions and intersections. Traditional Blue Economy development often relies on expanding production, attracting investment, and increasing sectoral output in a sustainable manner. Circular approaches diversify economic opportunities by creating value from materials previously considered waste. This can include transforming discarded fishing gear into new products, converting organic aquaculture waste into fertilizers, or repurposing decommissioned offshore equipment. These activities create new business niches, encourage innovation, and reduce the environmental costs associated with linear production models.

Social dimensions also illustrate areas of convergence. Traditional frameworks highlight job creation, community development, and inclusive participation in marine sectors. Circularity reinforces these goals by promoting local entrepreneurship, enhancing skills related to repair and refurbishment, and supporting community-led resource management. Coastal communities play an important role in monitoring waste flows, maintaining ecosystems, and developing small-scale circular enterprises. The intersection between social equity and circularity strengthens the resilience of livelihoods and diversifies income sources.

At the intersection of both frameworks lies a shared commitment to sustainable development. Both seek to protect marine ecosystems and ensure long-term resource availability. Traditional Blue Economy approaches provide the foundation for sustainable practices across sectors, while circularity advances the next step by reshaping how resources move through economic systems. Together, they offer complementary pathways for transitioning marine industries toward models that operate within ecological limits and support long-term prosperity for coastal societies.

Role of Ocean Health, Decarbonization, and Biodiversity in Circularity

Ocean health is central to circular approaches in marine and coastal systems, as healthy ecosystems support the natural processes that sustain economic activity, absorb waste, and maintain ecological stability. Degraded oceans reduce the capacity of ecosystems to perform essential functions such as nutrient cycling, carbon sequestration, and habitat provision. Circularity emphasizes the need to operate within ecological boundaries by minimizing pollution, improving waste management, and adopting practices that prevent further degradation. In marine sectors, this includes reducing nutrient runoff, limiting the release of hazardous substances, and improving the management of waste streams generated by fishing, aquaculture, shipping, and tourism. Maintaining ocean health also requires restoring areas affected by overexploitation, destructive practices, or climate change, creating the conditions necessary for long-term sustainability.

Decarbonization is closely linked to circularity because many marine industries remain dependent on fossil fuels, contributing to emissions that affect the climate and ocean systems. Shipping, offshore energy operations, fishing fleets, and coastal industries all rely on conventional fuels that contribute to greenhouse gas emissions and air pollution. Circularity seeks to reduce energy use through efficiency measures while promoting the integration of renewable marine energy sources such as offshore wind, wave, and tidal systems. Electrification of port operations, adoption of low-emission vessels, and optimization of marine logistics can further reduce reliance on fossil fuels. Decarbonization strategies also influence material choices, as industries are encouraged to shift to low-carbon materials, improve the durability of equipment, and reduce emissions associated with production and transportation.

Climate change impacts such as ocean warming, acidification, and sea level rise add urgency to the need for decarbonization within the Blue Economy. Circular practices support adaptation by strengthening ecosystems, reducing waste, and promoting resource-efficient systems that are less vulnerable to environmental disruption. When combined with renewable energy integration, circularity helps build a more resilient economic foundation that reduces exposure to climate-related risks. This is particularly important for coastal communities and marine industries that rely directly on stable environmental conditions.

Biodiversity plays a critical role in ensuring that marine ecosystems remain productive, resilient, and capable of supporting circular resource flows. High biodiversity enhances ecosystem functions such as water filtration, habitat formation, and nutrient regulation. These functions help maintain the quality and availability of ocean resources essential for fisheries, aquaculture, and other marine sectors. Circularity reinforces biodiversity conservation by reducing pollution, minimizing habitat disturbance, and designing systems that prevent or reduce harm to marine life. For example, gear modifications can reduce bycatch, while improved waste management prevents plastics and other debris from entering the ocean. Circular aquaculture systems reduce nutrient overload and limit the spread of invasive species.

The restoration of habitats such as mangroves, seagrasses, and coral reefs aligns with circular principles by strengthening ecosystem services that support both environmental and economic goals. These habitats store carbon, protect coastlines, and provide nursery areas for marine species. Restoring them also contributes to broader regenerative goals within circular frameworks. Habitat restoration supports fisheries productivity, enhances tourism opportunities, and safeguards the ecological functions that underpin the Blue Economy. In many regions, restoration efforts draw on traditional knowledge and community-based management practices, demonstrating the importance of local participation in maintaining biodiversity.

Integrated management approaches further highlight the connection between biodiversity, ocean health, and circularity. Marine spatial planning, ecosystem-based management, and environmental impact assessments help reduce conflicts between sectors and ensure that activities are aligned with ecological priorities. These tools support decisions about where and how industries operate, guiding the placement of renewable energy installations, aquaculture farms, and shipping routes. By aligning economic activities with ecological capacity, these approaches reduce cumulative impacts on biodiversity and support more efficient and sustainable resource use.

Technology and innovation contribute to maintaining ocean health and biodiversity within circular systems. Advances in monitoring, remote sensing, and environmental modelling provide better information about ecosystem conditions and resource flows. This enables industries and regulators to detect changes early, adapt practices promptly, and align operations with environmental thresholds. Digital tools also support traceability in supply chains, helping to ensure that products such as seafood are harvested sustainably and that waste is minimized. In restoration and conservation efforts, new techniques such as coral propagation, marine habitat reconstruction, and genetic research offer emerging opportunities to strengthen biodiversity.

The relationship between circularity, ocean health, decarbonization, and biodiversity reflects an interconnected system in which environmental conditions shape economic opportunities and long-term viability. Industries that depend on healthy oceans benefit from practices that reduce emissions, restore ecosystems, and protect marine life. In turn, circular strategies gain effectiveness when supported by strong environmental stewardship, technological advancement, and coordinated policy frameworks that reinforce ecological resilience.

Chapter 2: Governance and Policy Instruments Enabling Circularity

This chapter examines the governance frameworks, regulatory tools, and policy mechanisms that guide circular transitions in marine sectors. It highlights the role of international agreements, regional cooperation, and national strategies in shaping sustainable ocean management. The chapter also discusses how policy instruments can support innovation, strengthen compliance, and align economic activities with ecological limits.

International Frameworks: UNCLOS, SDG14, Kunming-Montreal GBF

International frameworks provide the foundation for governance approaches that support the transition toward circularity in marine and coastal systems. These frameworks establish legal obligations, policy goals, and cooperative mechanisms that guide how countries manage shared ocean resources. They also influence national legislation, marine spatial planning, conservation strategies, and the design of economic activities linked to the Blue Economy. By shaping expectations around sustainability, ecosystem protection, and resource efficiency, international agreements help align global efforts to integrate circular principles across marine sectors.

The United Nations Convention on the Law of the Sea (UNCLOS) remains the primary legal instrument governing the use of oceans and their resources. It defines the rights and responsibilities of states regarding maritime zones, navigation, fishing, environmental protection, and marine scientific research. UNCLOS sets out obligations to protect and preserve the marine environment, prevent pollution, and maintain living resources at sustainable levels. Its provisions encourage ecosystem-based management, pollution prevention measures, and cooperation on transboundary issues such as migratory species and shared fish stocks. While UNCLOS predates the emergence of circular economy concepts, its environmental obligations create a framework that supports efforts to reduce waste, improve resource stewardship, and restore degraded ecosystems. The agreement also provides the legal basis for port state controls and marine pollution regulations that align with circularity goals.

Sustainable Development Goal 14, focused on conserving and sustainably using oceans, seas, and marine resources, reinforces the importance of integrating environmental sustainability into marine economic activities. SDG 14 addresses issues such as marine pollution, sustainable fisheries, marine protected areas, ocean acidification, and the economic needs of small island and coastal developing states. Circularity aligns with these objectives by promoting waste reduction, resource efficiency, and ecosystem restoration. Targets related to reducing marine plastic pollution, enhancing scientific knowledge, and strengthening governance frameworks directly support circular approaches. The emphasis on sustainable economic benefits for coastal communities also aligns with circular business models that create value from recycled materials, resource recovery, and regenerative practices. SDG 14 operates within a wider framework of goals on climate action, responsible consumption and production, and biodiversity conservation, linking circularity to multiple areas of global development.

The Kunming-Montreal Global Biodiversity Framework (GBF) marks a significant step in strengthening international commitments to biodiversity protection and restoration. The framework sets targets for reducing pollution, protecting ecosystems, improving sustainable use, and mobilizing finance for biodiversity. Its goals emphasize a whole-of-society approach that involves governments, businesses, and communities in efforts to halt and reverse biodiversity loss. The GBF highlights the need to reduce nutrient pollution, eliminate harmful subsidies, and manage natural resources more sustainably. These priorities align with circularity by encouraging practices that reduce waste, prevent environmental degradation, and support ecosystem regeneration.

One of the key elements of the GBF is its focus on restoring degraded ecosystems and increasing conservation areas, including coastal and marine environments. Restoration efforts support circularity by enhancing the ecological foundations upon which marine industries depend, strengthening the resilience of ecosystems that provide essential services such as carbon sequestration, storm protection, and habitat provision. The framework encourages countries to integrate biodiversity considerations into economic planning, supply chains, and infrastructure development, creating opportunities for circular design standards, sustainable procurement, and nature-positive investments.

These international frameworks collectively shape the regulatory and policy environment in which circularity can advance. UNCLOS provides the legal structure for environmental protection and resource management, ensuring that activities in national waters and high seas are conducted responsibly. SDG 14 offers a global agenda that links economic development with environmental stewardship, creating incentives for reduction of waste and improved resource use. The Kunming-Montreal GBF strengthens commitments to protect and restore biodiversity, emphasizing the importance of ecosystems in supporting sustainable economies. Governments use these frameworks to inform national legislation, promote cross-border cooperation, and develop policies that integrate circular principles into marine strategies.

Regional Seas Conventions and National Marine Spatial Plans

Regional seas conventions provide cooperative frameworks for protecting marine and coastal environments across shared waters. These agreements enable countries within a geographic region to coordinate actions on pollution control, habitat protection, resource management, and monitoring. By addressing issues that cross national boundaries, regional seas conventions help harmonize standards and improve consistency across marine policies. Their mandates often include reducing pollution from land-based sources, improving waste management, regulating maritime activities, and

21

strengthening environmental governance. These areas directly support circularity by encouraging measures that limit waste, promote responsible resource use, and enhance environmental quality in marine ecosystems.

Many regional seas conventions include protocols that target specific pressures such as hazardous substances, nutrient runoff, oil spills, and marine litter. These protocols help establish common approaches to managing pollutants and preventing further degradation of coastal and offshore environments. Through shared guidelines, technical cooperation, and regional action plans, countries work together to improve environmental oversight and develop coordinated responses to emerging challenges. This cooperation supports the adoption of circular practices such as improving waste reception facilities, strengthening recycling systems, and enhancing monitoring of waste flows into marine environments. Regional conventions also provide platforms for research collaboration, capacity building, and knowledge exchange, helping countries adopt innovative approaches consistent with circular economy principles.

National marine spatial plans (MSPs) complement regional frameworks by providing structured processes for organizing the use of marine space within individual countries. MSPs aim to balance economic development, environmental protection, and social interests by guiding where and how activities occur in coastal and offshore areas. These plans consider ecological conditions, resource availability, existing uses, and future development needs. By mapping out zones for fishing, aquaculture, renewable energy, shipping routes, conservation areas, and tourism, MSPs reduce conflicts among sectors and improve long-term planning. Integrating circularity into MSPs involves identifying opportunities to reduce waste, enhance resource efficiency, and design marine activities that align with ecological limits.

Spatial planning helps ensure that economic activities do not exceed the carrying capacity of marine ecosystems. It supports the application of ecosystem-based management by incorporating information on habitats, species, and environmental processes into

22

decision-making. This approach guides the placement of infrastructure, such as offshore wind installations or aquaculture farms, in locations that minimize ecological impacts and promote efficient resource use. For example, MSPs can identify areas suitable for multi-use platforms that combine renewable energy production with aquaculture or other marine activities. Spatial planning can also guide the development of circular infrastructure, such as ports designed for waste segregation, recycling, and resource recovery.

MSPs increasingly incorporate climate considerations, recognizing that changing environmental conditions influence the sustainability of marine industries. Rising sea levels, ocean acidification, and shifting species distributions affect the viability of traditional uses and create new demands for spatial adaptation. Incorporating circular principles helps address these challenges by promoting designs and activities that reduce emissions, expand renewable energy use, and minimize ecological disturbance. Spatial plans that integrate decarbonization goals can support the development of offshore renewable energy projects, low-impact maritime transport routes, and coastal protection measures that rely on nature-based solutions.

Both regional seas conventions and national MSPs provide opportunities to integrate community participation and local knowledge into policy processes. Coastal populations often have strong cultural and economic connections to marine environments, making their involvement important for successful implementation. Public consultations, local advisory groups, and community-based monitoring programs contribute to more inclusive governance structures. Incorporating local knowledge can improve understanding of resource use patterns, environmental conditions, and potential conflicts among sectors. These inputs help refine circular strategies by ensuring they reflect local realities and support sustainable livelihoods.

The alignment of regional seas conventions and MSPs enhances governance coherence by linking cross-border environmental priorities with national-level planning and regulation. This coordination supports consistent application of circularity across marine sectors and strengthens the environmental basis for long-term economic development. As countries revise and update their spatial plans, the influence of regional commitments reinforces the importance of reducing waste, improving resource efficiency, and restoring degraded ecosystems within national jurisdictions.

Integrating Circular Economy into Marine Policies and Ocean Strategies

Integrating circular economy principles into marine policies and ocean strategies involves aligning regulatory frameworks, planning processes, and sectoral guidelines with approaches that reduce waste, improve resource efficiency, and support ecosystem regeneration. This integration requires governments to shift from managing individual environmental pressures to addressing the full life cycle of materials and activities associated with marine sectors. Circularity influences how policies are designed, how industries operate, and how national strategies prioritize sustainable development in coastal and offshore environments.

A key component of integrating circularity is the development of policy instruments that address upstream drivers of waste and resource use. Regulations can require improved product design, encourage eco-efficient technologies, and set standards for durability and reparability of equipment used in fisheries, aquaculture, and maritime industries. Policies may also promote the use of sustainable materials, reduce reliance on single-use plastics, and require producers to consider end-of-life management. Extended producer responsibility schemes can shift accountability for waste away from local governments and toward producers and importers, creating incentives for more circular design and product stewardship.

National marine strategies increasingly reflect these principles by highlighting the need for resource-efficient practices across coastal and marine sectors. Strategies may include targets for reducing pollution, improving recycling rates, and recovering resources from waste streams generated by maritime transport, ports, and coastal communities. In some countries, marine strategies link circularity with climate goals by promoting low-carbon materials, renewable energy integration, and the reduction of emissions across marine value chains. Policies may encourage the adoption of cleaner fuels, the electrification of port operations, and improvements in vessel efficiency, reducing both environmental impacts and operational costs.

Circularity also influences ocean strategies through the promotion of integrated management approaches. Ecosystem-based management, marine spatial planning, and watershed-scale coordination help reduce cumulative impacts on marine ecosystems. These tools enable policymakers to identify areas where circular initiatives can be deployed effectively, such as developing waste-to-resource hubs in coastal zones or locating processing facilities for marine byproducts near ports. Integrating circular economy principles into spatial planning can support co-location of activities, reduce transportation needs, and improve efficiency across marine industries.

Economic incentives form another pathway for integrating circularity. Governments can support circular approaches by providing grants, tax incentives, and low-interest loans for businesses that adopt resource-efficient technologies or create new circular products. Public procurement policies can prioritize goods and services that comply with circular standards, encouraging innovation across suppliers. Financial institutions may integrate circularity into blue finance instruments, enabling investments in projects that reduce waste, enhance recycling infrastructure, or support regenerative aquaculture practices. These economic measures help reduce barriers to adoption and foster the development of new markets based on circular principles.

Research, data collection, and monitoring systems support the integration of circularity by providing evidence for policy design and evaluation. Governments can invest in marine observation technologies, waste tracking systems, and life cycle assessment tools that allow policymakers to understand resource flows and identify areas where circular interventions are most effective. Improved data systems can also support transparency in seafood supply chains, strengthen enforcement of regulations, and improve international reporting on sustainability targets. Collaboration between governments, research institutions, and the private sector enhances the availability of knowledge needed to advance circular practices.

Education and capacity building contribute to the successful implementation of circular marine policies. Training programs for regulators, industry operators, and coastal communities help increase understanding of circular principles, regulatory requirements, and technical options for reducing waste. Universities, technical institutes, and vocational programs can incorporate circularity into curricula related to marine sciences, engineering, and environmental management. These efforts build a workforce capable of supporting the transition toward more sustainable marine industries.

Stakeholder engagement is vital for aligning marine policies with circular economy objectives. Coastal communities, Indigenous groups, industry associations, and non-governmental organizations play important roles in shaping strategies that reflect local priorities and environmental conditions. Participatory processes can help identify practical opportunities for circularity, improve compliance with regulations, and promote shared stewardship of marine resources. Engaging stakeholders early in policy development ensures that circular approaches are grounded in the realities of marine sectors and supported by those directly involved in their implementation.

Integrating circular economy principles into marine policies and ocean strategies ultimately depends on coordination across government ministries, sectors, and levels of governance. Fisheries, shipping, energy, tourism, waste management, and environmental agencies must work together to ensure coherent regulation and avoid policy conflicts. International cooperation further strengthens national efforts by providing access to expertise, harmonizing standards, and facilitating cross-border initiatives that support circularity in shared marine regions.

Role of Multilateral Development Banks and Regional Organizations

Multilateral development banks play an important role in advancing circularity within the Blue Economy by providing finance, technical assistance, and policy support that enable countries to adopt more sustainable marine practices. Their mandates focus on fostering economic development while addressing environmental risks, making them key actors in promoting investments that reduce waste, improve resource efficiency, and support ecosystem restoration. Through loans, grants, and blended finance instruments, these institutions help governments and private sector partners develop infrastructure and systems aligned with circular principles. This includes financing for waste management facilities in coastal areas, upgrading ports with circular design features, and supporting renewable marine energy projects.

In addition to financial support, multilateral development banks assist countries in strengthening regulatory and institutional frameworks. They help develop national strategies, policy reforms, and planning documents that incorporate circular economy principles into marine governance. This support often includes drafting guidelines for sustainable fisheries, improving environmental impact assessment processes, and integrating resource efficiency into marine spatial plans. By working directly with government agencies, banks contribute to building the capacity needed to manage marine resources more sustainably. Their involvement often helps align national priorities with international commitments related to climate mitigation, biodiversity conservation, and marine pollution reduction.

Technical assistance programs offered by multilateral development banks help countries adopt innovative technologies and management approaches. These programs can include pilot projects that test circular solutions, such as resource recovery from aquaculture waste or recycling systems for fishing gear. Banks may also support digital platforms that improve traceability in seafood supply chains or enhance monitoring of marine pollution. Through knowledge-sharing initiatives and regional workshops, they facilitate collaboration among countries facing similar challenges. This exchange of experience helps spread best practices and accelerates the adoption of circular approaches across different marine sectors.

Regional organizations complement the work of multilateral development banks by coordinating policy implementation across countries that share marine ecosystems. These organizations develop regional action plans, guidelines, and standards that address pollution control, habitat protection, and resource management. Their efforts support the harmonization of regulations, which is essential for managing transboundary issues such as marine litter, migratory fish stocks, and shipping emissions. Regional organizations often work through committees and working groups that bring together government representatives, researchers, and industry stakeholders to design solutions tailored to specific regional contexts.

Many regional organizations focus on strengthening marine governance and improving compliance with international agreements. They carry out monitoring activities, assess environmental conditions, and support enforcement efforts. This work enhances the effectiveness of circular initiatives by ensuring that waste reduction measures, pollution controls, and conservation efforts are applied consistently across borders. Regional partnerships also create opportunities for joint projects, such as shared recycling facilities, coordinated habitat restoration programs, or collaborative efforts to reduce abandoned, lost, or discarded fishing gear.

Capacity building is an important aspect of the work undertaken by regional organizations. They provide training programs, technical manuals, and advisory services that help countries improve their regulatory and technical capabilities. These initiatives support the implementation of circular practices at both national and local levels by enhancing knowledge about resource-efficient technologies, sustainable production methods, and monitoring techniques. Capacity-building efforts also help ensure that policies are effectively applied and maintained over time.

Regional organizations often serve as platforms for stakeholder engagement. They convene dialogues involving governments, civil society groups, and private sector actors, enabling broader participation in the development of circular strategies. This engagement helps identify practical solutions, address potential conflicts among sectors, and ensure that circular approaches consider social and economic dimensions. By including coastal communities, regional organizations help integrate traditional knowledge and local priorities into marine governance processes.

Partnerships between multilateral development banks and regional organizations strengthen the overall governance landscape for circularity in the Blue Economy. Banks provide financial and technical resources, while regional organizations offer contextual knowledge, coordination mechanisms, and policy structures that support collective action. Together, these institutions help countries adopt circular principles through a combination of investment, regulatory support, capacity building, and regional collaboration.

Chapter 3: Circular Business Models in Marine Sectors

This chapter explores circular business models that enable more efficient and regenerative use of marine resources. It outlines how key sectors such as fisheries, aquaculture, shipping, tourism, and biotechnology can adopt approaches that reduce waste and extend resource value. The chapter highlights opportunities for innovation and identifies structural challenges to implementation.

Overview of Circular Business Models

Circular business models provide mechanisms for reducing resource use, extending product life cycles, and creating value from materials that would otherwise be discarded. In marine and coastal sectors, these models help shift activities away from linear systems of extraction, production, and disposal toward approaches that keep resources circulating for longer periods. The application of circular business models in the Blue Economy involves adapting production processes, redesigning supply chains, and adopting new service-based offerings that reduce environmental impacts while supporting economic viability.

One of the key circular business models is product life extension, which focuses on maintaining, repairing, upgrading, or remanufacturing products so they remain in use for longer periods. In marine industries, this model applies to vessels, machinery, aquaculture infrastructure, and port equipment. Extending the life of assets reduces demand for new materials and minimizes the environmental footprint associated with manufacturing and disposal. Companies can offer maintenance services, refurbishment programs, and modular designs that allow equipment to be easily repaired or upgraded. Life extension also involves improving durability and ensuring that products can withstand the harsh conditions of marine environments.

Another circular business model is resource recovery, which involves capturing and reprocessing materials from waste streams to create new products or feedstocks. Marine sectors generate a range of waste materials, including plastics, metals, organic waste, and components from decommissioned infrastructure. Resource recovery can include recycling fishing gear, converting aquaculture byproducts into fertilizers or animal feed, and repurposing scrap materials from shipyards. Ports can serve as hubs for collecting and sorting marine waste, enabling more effective recycling and reducing the volume of materials entering the ocean. This model supports the development of secondary markets for recovered materials and reduces pressure on natural resources.

Product-as-a-service is a business model in which companies retain ownership of products and provide access or functionality as a service rather than selling the product outright. In the marine context, this model can apply to navigation equipment, monitoring devices, and machinery used in ports or offshore industries. By shifting from ownership to service-based arrangements, producers maintain responsibility for maintenance, repair, and end-of-life management. This creates incentives for designing durable, efficient, and easily recyclable products. It also reduces the need for customers to purchase new equipment, lowering material consumption across the sector. Subscription-based services, leasing models, and performance-based contracts all fall under this category.

Circular supply chains support business models by redesigning material flows, improving traceability, and incorporating sustainability considerations from the sourcing stage through production and end-of-life. In marine industries, circular supply chains promote the use of recycled or bio-based materials, ensure responsible sourcing of raw materials, and support transparency in product components. Digital tools such as blockchain can help track the origin, composition, and condition of products, facilitating reuse and recycling. Circular supply chains also enhance resilience by reducing dependence on finite resources and diversifying material inputs.

Industrial symbiosis is another circular model that enables different industries to share resources, infrastructure, or waste streams in ways that create mutual benefits. In coastal regions, waste from one marine sector can serve as a resource for another. For example, organic waste from seafood processing can be used in aquaculture feed or converted into bioenergy. Shared facilities, such as waste processing centers or renewable energy infrastructure, can reduce costs and improve efficiency across sectors. Industrial symbiosis encourages collaboration among businesses and supports the development of regional circular ecosystems.

Circular business models also include models focused on dematerialization and efficiency. These models use digital technologies to reduce the need for physical materials by optimizing operations. Smart systems can reduce fuel consumption in shipping, improve feed efficiency in aquaculture, and minimize waste in fisheries. By using data analytics, automation, and remote monitoring, companies can identify inefficiencies and adjust processes to reduce material and energy use.

Businesses adopting circular models often engage with consumers and stakeholders to promote sustainable practices. In marine tourism, operators may offer services that emphasize low-impact experiences, support local conservation efforts, or encourage recycling and waste reduction. In seafood supply chains, companies may engage consumers by offering products certified for sustainability or by providing transparent information on sourcing practices.

Taken together, these circular business models contribute to the development of economic activities that prioritize resource efficiency, waste reduction, and long-term sustainability across marine and coastal sectors.

Applications in Fisheries, Aquaculture, Shipping, Tourism, Biotechnology

Circular economy approaches are increasingly being applied across fisheries, aquaculture, shipping, tourism, and marine biotechnology to reduce waste, improve resource efficiency, and support more sustainable production systems. Each sector presents distinct opportunities for circularity based on its resource flows, environmental impacts, and technological capabilities. Integrating circular principles into these industries requires adjustments to business practices, regulatory frameworks, and supply chain operations.

In fisheries, circularity focuses on reducing waste throughout harvesting, processing, and distribution. Improvements in gear design can help reduce bycatch and prevent the loss of fishing equipment that contributes to marine litter. When gear does reach the end of its life, recycling programs can transform nets and ropes into new materials. Processing facilities can adopt resource recovery techniques to convert fish waste into valuable products such as fishmeal, oils, biofertilizers, and collagen. Traceability tools enhance transparency and support responsible sourcing, ensuring that fish stocks are harvested sustainably. Cold chain improvements reduce spoilage and extend product life, lowering overall resource demand. By integrating circular practices into fisheries management, resource use is optimized and environmental pressures are reduced.

Aquaculture systems offer opportunities to apply circular approaches to feed inputs, nutrient cycles, and waste streams. Integrated multi-trophic aquaculture pairs species that use different parts of the food web, allowing waste from one species to serve as input for another. This reduces environmental impacts and increases overall productivity. Circular strategies also include shifting to alternative feeds such as insect protein, algae, or microbial sources, reducing dependence on wild-caught fish for fishmeal and fish oil. Wastewater treatment technologies can capture nutrients from aquaculture effluent, enabling recovery of materials such as nitrogen and phosphorus. These materials can be repurposed into fertilizers or other products. Advancements in closed-loop systems allow for more controlled environments, reducing water use and preventing the release of waste into surrounding ecosystems.

In shipping, circularity focuses on improving energy efficiency, reducing emissions, and managing materials used in vessels and port operations. Cleaner propulsion technologies, including electrification, hydrogen, ammonia, and advanced biofuels, support decarbonization while increasing operational efficiency. Vessel design improvements enable easier maintenance and disassembly, allowing materials such as steel and other metals to be recovered at the end of a ship's life. Ports play an important role by providing waste reception facilities, supporting recycling, and enabling circular supply chains that connect maritime industries with resource recovery systems. Digital tools help optimize routes, monitor fuel use, and reduce operational waste. Retrofitting older vessels extends their lifespan and reduces the need for new construction, aligning with circular principles of product life extension.

Marine tourism can integrate circular practices through waste reduction, sustainable infrastructure, and nature-positive experiences. Tourism operators can adopt resource-efficient accommodations, reduce single-use plastics, and improve waste collection systems in coastal areas. Circularity also extends to the design of tourism facilities, which may use durable materials, modular structures, and renewable energy. Activities offered by tourism companies can support conservation efforts, engage communities, and promote environmental awareness. Cruise tourism presents additional challenges, but circular approaches can help improve waste management, reduce energy consumption, and enhance recycling onboard. Tourism's influence on consumer behavior creates opportunities to reinforce circular practices more broadly.

Marine biotechnology supports circularity by developing bio-based materials and processes that reduce reliance on non-renewable resources. Biotechnology companies can convert marine biomass, such as algae, into sustainable products including bioplastics, pharmaceuticals, cosmetics, and nutraceuticals. Algae capture carbon and require fewer inputs compared to land-based crops, making them suitable for circular production systems. Biotechnology also supports waste valorization by transforming byproducts from fisheries and aquaculture into high-value compounds. Enzymatic processes, microbial fermentation, and advanced extraction methods enable efficient use of marine biomass. Research and innovation in this sector contribute to the development of materials and products designed for biodegradability, durability, and reduced environmental impact.

The application of circular principles across these sectors is supported by digitalization, policy frameworks, and market incentives. Technologies such as sensors, blockchain, and remote monitoring help track resource use and improve efficiency. Regulations can encourage sustainable design, responsible sourcing, and waste recovery. Market demand for environmentally responsible products and services further incentivizes industries to adopt circular practices. As circular approaches become more integrated into fisheries, aquaculture, shipping, tourism, and biotechnology, they help shape marine economies that are more resilient, efficient, and aligned with long-term environmental goals.

Private Sector Innovation and Cross-Sector Partnerships

Private sector innovation is a driving force in the transition toward circularity within the Blue Economy. Businesses are developing technologies, services, and operational models that reduce waste, optimize resource use, and support regenerative marine practices. These innovations arise from the need to comply with regulatory requirements, respond to market expectations, and improve long-term resilience. Companies in fisheries, aquaculture, shipping, tourism, and marine biotechnology are adopting advanced tools that enhance efficiency, minimize environmental impacts, and create new value streams from materials previously considered waste.

In fisheries and aquaculture, private sector initiatives include the development of eco-designed gear aimed at reducing bycatch and preventing gear loss. Innovations in biodegradable materials help reduce the environmental footprint of nets, traps, and buoys.

Businesses are implementing digital tracking systems that monitor gear location, improving retrieval rates and reducing marine litter. In aquaculture, firms are adopting smart feeding systems, automated monitoring platforms, and sensors that optimize inputs and reduce waste. These innovations contribute to resource efficiency and help producers meet sustainability standards required by international supply chains.

Shipping companies are investing in cleaner propulsion technologies, advanced hull coatings, and energy-efficient vessel designs. These innovations reduce fuel consumption and extend the operational life of ships. Private firms are adopting digital platforms that optimize route planning, improve cargo handling efficiency, and monitor emissions in real time. Ports are collaborating with maritime technology providers to install shore power systems, support renewable energy integration, and enhance waste reception facilities. Such investments by the private sector align with circular principles by lowering emissions and enabling better management of materials throughout a vessel's life cycle.

In marine tourism, private operators are integrating circular practices into facility design, waste management, and service delivery. Hotels and resorts in coastal areas are adopting water-efficient technologies, renewable energy systems, and waste-sorting infrastructure. Tour operators introduce low-impact activities that educate visitors and support local conservation efforts. Cruise companies are adopting onboard waste reduction systems, recycling protocols, and advanced wastewater treatment technologies. These innovations contribute to resource efficiency and help mitigate environmental pressures in popular coastal destinations.

Marine biotechnology firms are advancing the development of bio-based materials, sustainable feed alternatives, and value-added products derived from marine biomass. Private companies are producing biodegradable polymers from algae, transforming fisheries byproducts into high-value ingredients, and exploring microbial processes that convert organic waste into useful compounds. These innovations reduce dependency on non-renewable materials and support the creation of circular value chains. Research partnerships with universities and research institutions help accelerate innovation and bring new products to market.

Cross-sector partnerships strengthen these private initiatives by linking industries, governments, research institutions, and civil society organizations. Collaboration allows different actors to share knowledge, pool resources, and address challenges that cannot be solved within a single sector. Many circular solutions require coordinated action, such as recovering marine litter, developing shared infrastructure, or creating regional markets for recycled materials. Partnerships between fisheries cooperatives, waste management companies, and technology providers help establish systems for collecting and recycling fishing gear. In aquaculture, collaboration with feed companies, environmental organizations, and research institutions supports the development of sustainable feed alternatives and closed-loop nutrient systems.

Public-private partnerships facilitate investment in infrastructure such as recycling plants, waste reception facilities, and renewable energy installations. Governments can provide enabling conditions through regulatory frameworks, financial incentives, and technical guidance, while private actors deliver expertise, operational capacity, and market access. When aligned, these partnerships help scale circular solutions and integrate them into mainstream marine economies. Cross-sector collaboration is also essential for implementing marine spatial planning, ecosystem-based management, and regional strategies that aim to balance ecological and economic priorities.

Non-governmental organizations contribute by mediating dialogue, monitoring environmental performance, and supporting community engagement. Partnerships involving local communities ensure that circular solutions reflect local conditions, build on traditional knowledge, and enhance livelihood resilience. Industry associations play a role in setting standards, disseminating best practices, and coordinating initiatives across supply chains. When industries work together, they can create unified approaches that facilitate broader adoption of circular principles.

Financing platforms and accelerators support private innovation through grants, equity investment, and advisory services. These organizations help startups and established companies develop circular products, scale their operations, and enter new markets. Collaboration with multilateral development banks and regional organizations strengthens access to funding and technical assistance for circular investments in coastal and marine sectors.

Through innovation and cross-sector collaboration, the private sector contributes to the development of systems that reduce waste, improve resource efficiency, and support ecosystem regeneration across the Blue Economy.

Barriers: Finance, Regulation, Cultural Resistance

Implementing circular approaches in the Blue Economy faces several barriers related to financial constraints, regulatory limitations, and cultural resistance within industries and communities. These challenges can slow the adoption of new technologies, hinder investment in sustainable infrastructure, and limit the willingness of stakeholders to modify established practices. Addressing these barriers requires coordinated action across government, industry, and society to create conditions that support circular solutions in marine and coastal sectors.

Financial barriers stem from the upfront costs associated with adopting circular technologies, upgrading infrastructure, and modifying production systems. Many marine industries operate with narrow profit margins, making it difficult to allocate resources toward long-term sustainability investments. Circular solutions such as waste recovery facilities, renewable energy integration, and durable product design often require significant capital expenditure before generating economic returns. Small and medium-sized enterprises may face additional challenges in accessing finance due to limited collateral, higher perceived risk, or a lack of tailored financial products. Even when long-term cost savings are evident, uncertainty about market demand or resource availability can deter investment. Financial institutions may be hesitant to support projects involving untested technologies or new business models, particularly in regions with limited regulatory stability or technical capacity.

Regulatory barriers arise when existing policies are not designed to support circular practices or inadvertently reinforce linear models. Many marine regulations focus on managing impacts rather than redesigning systems to prevent waste or promote resource recovery. In some cases, permitting processes do not allow the flexible reuse of materials, creating obstacles for businesses seeking to repurpose equipment or recycle end-of-life components. Regulatory inconsistencies across jurisdictions also hinder cross-border circular value chains, especially in areas managed through regional seas agreements. Waste classification rules may complicate the transport of recovered materials, while subsidies for conventional practices can reduce the competitiveness of circular alternatives. The lack of standards for recycled materials or sustainable product design limits the ability of industries to adopt circular products at scale. Addressing these regulatory gaps requires updating policies to reflect circular principles and creating harmonized frameworks that encourage innovation.

Cultural resistance represents another barrier, particularly in traditional sectors such as fisheries and shipping, where long-standing practices and norms can slow the adoption of new approaches. In some cases, operators may be skeptical about the reliability or practicality of circular technologies, especially if they involve unfamiliar methods or require changes to daily routines. Resistance may also stem from concerns about costs, productivity, or regulatory compliance. Communities that rely on established resource use patterns may be reluctant to shift toward new models if they perceive risks to their livelihoods or cultural practices. In coastal areas, waste separation and recycling may be viewed as burdensome without adequate infrastructure or incentives. Consumer expectations also influence market dynamics, as demand for low-cost products can discourage businesses from investing in higher-quality, durable, or repairable alternatives.

Capacity gaps contribute to cultural resistance by limiting awareness of circular opportunities. Where technical knowledge is limited, businesses may not fully understand the benefits of resource efficiency, product life extension, or waste recovery. Training programs and knowledge-sharing platforms can help address these gaps, but their reach varies across regions. Without adequate education and support, stakeholders may perceive circularity as complex or unfeasible within their specific operational contexts. Communication challenges also arise when the terminology of circular economy frameworks does not align with the practical language used in marine industries.

Infrastructure limitations reinforce other barriers by making circular practices difficult to implement. In many coastal regions, waste management systems lack the capacity to collect, sort, or process materials for recycling. Ports may not have adequate facilities for handling waste from ships or aquaculture operations. Limited access to renewable energy or modern technology can hinder the deployment of circular solutions. These constraints disproportionately affect remote or developing coastal areas, creating inequalities in the adoption of circular practices across regions.

Market barriers can also slow progress. For circular products and services to succeed, there must be stable demand, reliable supply chains, and clear pricing signals. Markets for recycled marine materials, repurposed equipment, or biobased products are still emerging in many regions. Without established buyers, companies may struggle to justify investments in resource recovery systems. Variability in the quality of recovered materials can further complicate the development of stable markets.

Overcoming these barriers involves mobilizing finance, updating regulations, improving infrastructure, and supporting cultural change. Governments, industry associations, and financial institutions each play important roles in creating enabling conditions for circularity across the Blue Economy.

Chapter 4: Sustainable Fisheries and Aquaculture Through Circular Approaches

This chapter focuses on how circular practices enhance sustainability in fisheries and aquaculture. It examines strategies that improve resource efficiency, reduce environmental impacts, and support ecosystem regeneration. The chapter highlights the potential of integrated systems, improved traceability, and alternative feed sources to strengthen long-term viability.

Circularity in Fish Stock Management, Byproduct Valorization, and Closed-Loop Aquaculture Systems

Circularity in fish stock management involves aligning harvesting practices with ecosystem dynamics to maintain healthy populations and reduce waste throughout the supply chain. This approach includes improving stock assessments, strengthening monitoring systems, and adopting selective fishing techniques that minimize bycatch. Gear modifications, such as using materials designed to reduce lost fishing equipment, help prevent additional environmental impacts. Circularity also supports the use of digital tools that track catch composition, vessel activity, and stock conditions, enabling more precise management decisions. By improving efficiency and reducing discard rates, fish stock management becomes more aligned with resource conservation and long-term sustainability.

Byproduct valorization transforms materials that were previously discarded into useful products. During fish processing, significant quantities of heads, bones, skins, and viscera are generated. These materials can be converted into fishmeal, fish oil, collagen, bioactive compounds, and fertilizers through modern processing technologies. Valorization reduces waste volumes, creates new revenue streams, and enhances overall resource efficiency. Advances in biochemical processing allow producers to extract high-value ingredients for pharmaceuticals, cosmetics, and nutraceuticals. Integrating valorization into seafood processing supports a more holistic use of harvested resources and reduces the environmental footprint associated with disposal.

Closed-loop aquaculture systems further advance circularity by reusing water, capturing waste, and maintaining controlled environments that limit external impacts. Recirculating aquaculture systems filter and treat water for repeated use, significantly reducing water consumption and preventing nutrient-rich effluent from entering surrounding ecosystems. Solid waste can be processed into valuable byproducts, while dissolved nutrients can support the cultivation of aquatic plants or algae. Integrated multi-trophic aquaculture pairs species in complementary roles, allowing waste from one organism to serve as input for another. These systems help optimize resource flows and reduce dependency on external inputs.

Closed-loop approaches are supported by technological innovations such as real-time monitoring, automated feeding systems, and advanced filtration methods. These tools help operators optimize conditions for growth while minimizing inefficiencies. The use of alternative feed sources, including algae, insects, and microbial proteins, reduces pressure on wild fish stocks and aligns aquaculture operations with circular principles. Through improved system design, nutrient recovery, and sustainable feed development, closed-loop aquaculture contributes to more responsible and efficient production models in the Blue Economy.

Closed-Loop Aquaculture and Integrated Multi-Trophic Systems

Closed-loop aquaculture systems apply circular principles by minimizing inputs, reducing waste, and creating controlled environments that limit ecological impacts. These systems, often known as recirculating aquaculture systems, continuously filter and reuse water, significantly reducing the volume withdrawn from natural sources. Filtration units remove solids, convert ammonia to less harmful compounds, and maintain water quality through mechanical, biological, and chemical processes. This approach allows producers to maintain stable growing conditions, improve biosecurity, and reduce the risk of disease outbreaks. By containing effluent and preventing nutrient discharge into surrounding ecosystems, closed-loop systems support more sustainable and predictable production.

A central component of closed-loop aquaculture is waste capture and utilization. Solid waste collected through filtration can be processed into fertilizers or used as a feedstock for anaerobic digestion to generate biogas. Dissolved nutrients can be recovered through treatment technologies that precipitate compounds such as phosphorus or convert nitrogen into usable forms. These recovered materials can support agricultural applications or be used to cultivate algae or aquatic plants. Capturing and reusing waste aligns production with circularity by transforming byproducts into valuable resources rather than allowing them to enter waterways.

Water efficiency is another advantage of closed-loop systems. By continuously recycling water, these systems reduce overall consumption and lessen reliance on freshwater resources. This is particularly valuable in regions where water scarcity affects agricultural and industrial sectors. The ability to operate with minimal water exchange also reduces exposure to pollutants and pathogens present in open environments. Enhanced control over water parameters enables more consistent growth rates, improves survival, and supports higher-density production compared to traditional methods.

Integrated multi-trophic aquaculture is an approach that combines multiple species with complementary functions within a single system. Species are selected based on their roles in nutrient cycling, creating a production environment that mimics ecological relationships found in natural ecosystems. Finfish or shellfish generate organic waste that serves as an input for other organisms. Filter feeders such as mussels can remove suspended particles from the water, while seaweed or other aquatic plants absorb dissolved nutrients. These interactions create a balanced system that reduces environmental impacts and increases overall productivity.

The structure of integrated multi-trophic aquaculture varies depending on species selection, environmental conditions, and desired products. In coastal systems, seaweeds may be cultivated near fish cages to absorb excess nutrients, while shellfish farms can help maintain water clarity. In freshwater environments, combinations of fish, crustaceans, and aquatic plants can be tailored to local conditions. The success of these systems depends on carefully matching species to ensure that nutrient flows are balanced and that each organism contributes to overall system stability.

Integrated multi-trophic aquaculture enhances resource efficiency by converting waste streams into revenue-generating products. Seaweed can be sold for food, cosmetics, pharmaceuticals, or biofuel production. Shellfish produced in these systems support local markets and require no external feed inputs. Plants grown in nutrient-rich waters may be used in aquaculture feeds or other value-added products. The diversification of outputs reduces financial risk for producers and increases the resilience of aquaculture operations.

Technological advancements further support the integration of closed-loop approaches and multi-trophic systems. Real-time monitoring tools track water quality, nutrient levels, and biological performance, enabling operators to adjust conditions as needed. Automated feeding systems respond to behavioral cues from fish to reduce feed waste. Sensors and data analytics improve system efficiency by optimizing resource flows, reducing energy consumption, and preventing system failures.

Feed innovation also plays a role in advancing circular aquaculture. Traditional feeds rely heavily on fishmeal and fish oil derived from wild stocks, creating pressures on marine ecosystems. Alternative feed sources such as insect meal, algae, microbial proteins, and agricultural byproducts reduce dependence on wild-caught inputs. When combined with closed-loop and integrated systems, these feeds contribute to more sustainable production and better alignment with circular principles.

Regulatory frameworks influence the adoption of these systems by setting standards for water quality, biosecurity, and waste management. Supportive policies can encourage investment in closed-loop technologies and streamline licensing for integrated systems. Financial incentives, technical assistance, and research partnerships help address barriers related to cost, expertise, and infrastructure. Collaboration among governments, producers, researchers, and technology providers strengthens the conditions needed to expand circular aquaculture.

Closed-loop aquaculture and integrated multi-trophic systems exemplify how circular principles can be applied to enhance efficiency, reduce environmental impacts, and diversify outputs. Through system design, waste recovery, nutrient recycling, and species integration, these approaches contribute to more sustainable and resilient aquaculture models.

Traceability, Digital Tools, and Sustainable Feed Alternatives

Traceability systems are an essential component of circular approaches in fisheries and aquaculture, as they provide transparency across the supply chain and improve the reliability of sustainability claims. Effective traceability enables stakeholders to monitor the movement of products from harvest or cultivation through processing, transportation, and retail. Digital platforms such as electronic catch documentation, barcodes, and blockchain technologies help record data on origin, handling practices, and product quality. These systems support compliance with sustainability standards, reduce the risk of illegal or unreported fishing, and improve consumer confidence. By improving data flow and reducing uncertainty, traceability strengthens the foundation for resource-efficient production and responsible management of marine resources.

Digital tools enhance operational efficiency in both fisheries and aquaculture by enabling real-time monitoring and more precise decision-making. Sensors placed on vessels or in aquaculture facilities can track water quality, temperature, oxygen levels, feeding behavior, and fish health metrics. These tools support automatic adjustments that reduce waste and improve overall productivity. For example, automated feeding systems use behavioral cues to determine appropriate feed quantities, minimizing overfeeding and limiting nutrient pollution. In fisheries, vessel monitoring systems and satellite tracking help optimize routes, reduce fuel consumption, and provide insight into fishing patterns. Digital modeling tools can also predict stock behavior and environmental conditions, improving stock assessments and supporting adaptive management.

Remote monitoring and data analytics play an important role in reducing losses across the value chain. Early detection of disease outbreaks in aquaculture facilities can prevent mass mortality events and reduce the need for chemical treatments. Predictive analytics help operators anticipate maintenance needs for equipment, enabling timely interventions that reduce downtime and prevent material waste. In processing facilities, digital quality control systems ensure better handling and reduce spoilage. These tools increase the efficiency of resource use and support greater alignment with circular principles by reducing waste at multiple stages of production.

Sustainable feed alternatives represent another major area of innovation in circular aquaculture. Conventional feeds rely heavily on fishmeal and fish oil derived from wild-caught fish, creating pressure on marine ecosystems. Developing alternative feed ingredients helps reduce dependency on wild stocks and supports more circular, resilient production systems. Insect meal produced from species such as black soldier flies offers a high-protein alternative that requires fewer resources to produce and can be grown on organic waste. Algae-based feeds provide long-chain omega-3 fatty acids without relying on forage fish. Microbial proteins grown through fermentation processes offer another promising alternative, requiring limited land or water.

Agricultural byproducts, such as oilseed cakes or plant-based proteins, are also increasingly incorporated into aquaculture feeds. When sourced responsibly, these ingredients reduce reliance on marine resources and support circularity by utilizing materials that might otherwise be discarded or underused. Continuous research is improving the nutritional profile and digestibility of plant-based feeds, making them more viable for a wider range of aquaculture species. Blended feeds that combine multiple alternative ingredients are being developed to achieve balanced nutritional content while reducing environmental impacts.

Waste streams from fisheries and aquaculture can also serve as inputs for feed production. Byproducts such as trimmings, offcuts, and fish frames can be processed into fishmeal and fish oil for aquaculture use. This approach reduces waste, increases resource efficiency, and lowers the demand for new raw materials. Innovations in enzymatic processing and fermentation allow producers to extract higher-value compounds from these waste streams, improving feed quality while supporting circular value chains. Using locally available byproducts can also reduce transportation-related emissions.

Digital tools complement the adoption of sustainable feed alternatives by monitoring feed efficiency and environmental impacts. Systems that track feed conversion ratios, nutrient retention, and waste outputs help producers adjust feed strategies to minimize inputs. Data collected from these tools supports ongoing research into alternative feeds and helps refine formulations to match species-specific nutritional needs. Transparent reporting systems improve communication with consumers and regulators, supporting the broader transition toward sustainable aquaculture.

Collaboration among feed producers, researchers, farmers, and technology providers accelerates innovation in sustainable feed development. Joint initiatives support the scaling of new technologies, improve cost competitiveness, and ensure that feed formulations meet the nutritional requirements of different species. Policy support, including incentives for research and standards for sustainable feed production, helps create the conditions needed for widespread adoption.

Together, traceability systems, digital tools, and sustainable feed alternatives strengthen circular approaches in fisheries and aquaculture by improving transparency, reducing waste, and lowering environmental pressures associated with feed production.

Local and Indigenous Knowledge Systems

Local and Indigenous knowledge systems contribute valuable insights to circular practices in fisheries and aquaculture by offering deep understanding of marine environments, species behavior, and ecosystem dynamics. These knowledge systems are rooted in long-term interactions with coastal and marine ecosystems and often emphasize stewardship, balance, and resource renewal. They provide practical guidance on sustainable harvesting, seasonal patterns, and environmental changes that may not always be captured through scientific monitoring alone. Incorporating this knowledge into management frameworks strengthens the ecological foundation of circular approaches and supports more adaptive decision-making.

Indigenous fishing practices often include selective harvesting methods that minimize waste and reduce impacts on non-target species. Traditional gear designs, such as traps and handlines, allow for targeted capture and reduce bycatch. In some communities, customary rules govern when and where fishing can occur, ensuring that sensitive habitats or breeding grounds are protected. These practices align with circular principles by maintaining ecosystem integrity and supporting long-term resource availability. Seasonal closures, rotational harvesting, and restrictions on certain species at particular life stages reflect an understanding of ecological cycles that supports sustainable stock management.

Local knowledge also informs habitat restoration and conservation efforts. Communities with long-standing connections to coastal environments often have detailed records of changes in water quality, species abundance, and ocean conditions. This information helps identify areas requiring restoration or protection and guides the selection of appropriate methods. In regions where mangroves, seagrasses, and other coastal habitats have been degraded, community-led restoration initiatives draw on traditional practices for planting, site selection, and long-term maintenance. These efforts contribute to ecosystem regeneration and complement scientific approaches.

In aquaculture, Indigenous and local practices offer insights into species behavior, water management, and integrated production systems. Traditional forms of aquaculture, such as fishponds, clam gardens, and coastal enclosures, demonstrate how communities historically managed nutrient cycles, minimized waste, and enhanced productivity through natural processes. These systems often rely on complementary relationships among species and on careful attention to water flow, tidal cycles, and seasonal variation. Modern applications of integrated multi-trophic aquaculture draw inspiration from these traditional methods by combining species that utilize different parts of the food web.

Local and Indigenous perspectives also influence the selection and use of materials. In many regions, traditional constructions for fishing gear or aquaculture structures use natural, biodegradable materials that reduce the risk of long-term pollution. These materials can be locally sourced, reducing dependency on imported inputs and lowering the environmental footprint of production. When integrated with contemporary design principles, traditional materials offer opportunities for innovation in low-impact gear and infrastructure suited to local conditions.

Knowledge transmission within communities supports circularity by reinforcing values of stewardship, sharing, and responsible resource use. Practices such as communal decision-making, shared access, and collective monitoring contribute to transparent and inclusive management. Local governance systems, including customary marine tenure arrangements, can regulate access to fishing grounds and reduce competition for resources. These structures create incentives for maintaining ecosystem health and stewarding resources for future generations.

The integration of local and Indigenous knowledge with scientific research enhances the effectiveness of circular strategies. Collaborative monitoring programs allow communities and scientists to compare observations, identify trends, and respond to environmental changes more quickly. Joint management arrangements formalize these partnerships and enable knowledge exchange. This collaboration supports adaptive management approaches that recognize the value of diverse knowledge sources.

Policy frameworks increasingly acknowledge the importance of Indigenous and local knowledge in marine resource management. Legal recognition of customary rights, co-management agreements, and participatory planning processes help ensure that these knowledge systems are respected and incorporated into decision-making. Involving communities in policy development strengthens compliance and facilitates the adoption of circular practices that reflect local needs and priorities.

Local and Indigenous enterprises contribute to circular economies by developing value-added products, restoration services, and community-based monitoring initiatives. Small-scale processing of byproducts, the creation of sustainable tourism opportunities, and involvement in habitat restoration projects provide economic benefits while reinforcing ecological stewardship. These activities support diversified livelihoods and increase the resilience of coastal communities to environmental and economic changes.

Local and Indigenous knowledge systems offer models of sustainable interaction with marine environments that complement scientific and technological approaches. Their integration into modern fisheries and aquaculture governance supports practices that enhance resource efficiency, maintain ecological balance, and strengthen the cultural foundations of coastal communities.

Chapter 5: Waste Management and Marine Litter Solutions

This chapter analyzes circular approaches to reducing marine pollution and improving coastal waste systems. It explores solutions such as enhanced waste collection, recycling, and resource recovery, as well as technologies that support debris monitoring and removal. The chapter emphasizes the importance of integrated systems that prevent waste from entering marine environments.

Marine Plastic Pollution and Circular Responses

Marine plastic pollution has become a significant environmental challenge affecting oceans, coastlines, and marine life. Plastics enter the marine environment from land-based sources, maritime activities, inadequate waste management systems, and lost or abandoned fishing gear. Once in the ocean, plastics fragment into microplastics, which disperse widely and accumulate in water columns, sediments, and the food web. These materials persist for decades or centuries, causing harm to marine species through ingestion, entanglement, and habitat disruption. The scale and complexity of marine plastic pollution highlight the need for systemic approaches that address both the sources and pathways of waste entering the ocean.

Circular responses aim to prevent plastics from becoming waste, improve material recovery, and minimize environmental leakage. Reducing plastic consumption is a central component of circularity, achieved through product redesign, substitution with alternative materials, and adoption of reusable systems. In coastal communities, measures such as limiting single-use plastics, promoting refill schemes, and encouraging the use of biodegradable or compostable materials help decrease the volume of waste entering waterways. Redesigning products for durability and ease of recycling supports longer material life cycles and reduces dependency on virgin plastic production.

Improving waste management infrastructure is essential for preventing marine plastic pollution. Many coastal regions struggle with inadequate collection systems, limited recycling capacity, and insufficient disposal facilities. Strengthening waste collection, expanding recycling operations, and developing facilities for processing different plastic types reduce the likelihood that waste will reach the marine environment. Ports play a key role by offering waste reception facilities that enable vessels to offload waste responsibly. Establishing clear protocols for sorting and handling waste in both urban and rural coastal areas supports more efficient and effective recycling systems.

Extended producer responsibility schemes encourage manufacturers to take responsibility for the end-of-life management of their products. These schemes require producers to contribute to the collection, recycling, or safe disposal of plastic materials they place on the market. By shifting responsibility to producers, such policies create incentives for designing products that are easier to recycle and generate less waste. Deposit-return programs for beverage containers also help improve collection rates and reduce litter in coastal areas.

Circular responses to marine plastic pollution include the development of markets for recycled marine plastics. Collecting and recycling plastics recovered from beaches, ports, and fishing activities provide materials for new products. Companies are increasingly incorporating recycled marine plastics into textiles, packaging, and consumer goods. This creates demand for recovered materials and encourages investment in collection and recycling systems. Innovations in chemical recycling offer opportunities to transform mixed or contaminated plastics into high-quality feedstocks suitable for a range of applications.

Efforts to address fishing gear loss are another significant component of circular strategies. Lost or abandoned fishing gear continues to trap marine species and contribute to long-term environmental impacts. Circular approaches promote the design of more durable or biodegradable gear, gear tracking technologies, and retrieval programs. Ports can establish collection points for end-of-life gear, enabling recycling or repurposing. Some initiatives transform recovered gear into new products such as flooring materials, construction components, or textiles.

Monitoring and cleanup efforts support circular strategies by identifying hotspots of plastic accumulation and informing targeted interventions. Remote sensing, drones, and oceanographic modelling help track the movement of floating plastics. Community-led beach cleanups and citizen science programs contribute valuable data on pollution patterns and provide immediate reductions in coastal litter. While cleanup efforts do not replace prevention, they help restore ecosystems and raise awareness of pollution sources.

Education and communication campaigns strengthen circular responses by promoting responsible behavior among consumers, industries, and communities. These initiatives highlight the consequences of improper waste disposal and encourage participation in reduction, reuse, and recycling efforts. Partnerships involving governments, non-governmental organizations, and private companies help amplify messages and reach diverse audiences.

Cooperation across sectors and borders is critical due to the transboundary nature of marine plastic pollution. Regional action plans, international agreements, and cross-border initiatives help align policies and coordinate activities aimed at reducing plastic leakage. Collaborative research efforts improve understanding of plastic distribution, ecological impacts, and effective mitigation strategies.

Marine plastic pollution requires integrated solutions that address production, consumption, waste management, and recovery. Circular responses help reduce environmental pressures by promoting resource efficiency, improving waste systems, and supporting product redesign.

Port Reception Facilities, EPR, and Deposit-Return Schemes

Port reception facilities support circular practices by providing designated areas where vessels can offload waste safely and efficiently. These facilities handle a range of materials, including plastics, oily residues, sewage, and discarded fishing gear. By ensuring that ships have reliable access to waste disposal services, ports reduce the likelihood that waste will be discharged into the ocean. Effective port reception systems require adequate capacity, clear operational procedures, and coordination among port authorities, waste management companies, and maritime operators. Transparent fee structures and streamlined reporting processes also encourage compliance and reduce operational delays for vessels.

Upgrading reception facilities can enhance the quality of waste segregation and improve recycling outcomes. Ports that implement sorting stations, compactors, and washing units enable cleaner streams of recyclable materials, making it easier for downstream processors to convert waste into new products. Integrating digital tools for waste tracking helps ports monitor volumes, identify patterns, and improve service delivery. Collaboration with local authorities ensures that collected waste enters appropriate recycling or treatment pathways rather than being directed to landfills with limited recovery options.

Extended producer responsibility schemes shift part of the burden for managing plastic waste from governments to manufacturers. Under these schemes, producers contribute financially or operationally to the collection and recycling of products once they reach end of life. In marine contexts, this applies to fishing gear, packaging materials, and products commonly used in coastal communities. By making producers responsible for the full life cycle of their goods, extended producer responsibility creates incentives for designing products that are more durable, less harmful, and easier to recycle.

Extended producer responsibility systems also support the development of specialized recycling programs for gear and other marine-related products. When producers are obligated to participate in or fund these programs, the likelihood of gear being returned, collected, and repurposed increases. Such schemes can stimulate innovation in gear design, promote biodegradable alternatives, and reduce the accumulation of waste in marine environments. Governments may complement these efforts with mandatory reporting requirements or labeling standards that improve transparency and traceability.

Deposit-return schemes are another important circular policy tool that helps reduce litter and increase recycling rates. These schemes add a small deposit to the purchase price of items such as beverage containers, fishing gear, or other products frequently found in coastal waste streams. Consumers or operators receive the deposit back when they return the item to a designated collection point. Deposit-return systems reduce litter by creating a financial incentive for recovery and support high-quality recycling by ensuring that returned items are clean and sorted.

In coastal regions, deposit-return schemes can be adapted to address items unique to marine settings. For example, programs may offer rewards for returning end-of-life nets or retrieving lost gear. Ports and coastal communities can host collection points where fishers drop off used equipment in exchange for a deposit refund. These approaches reduce the amount of gear entering the ocean and support the development of circular value chains for recovered materials.

Integrating port reception facilities, extended producer responsibility schemes, and deposit-return systems strengthens circular marine waste management. These tools address different stages of the product life cycle and involve multiple stakeholders, from producers and ports to consumers and coastal communities. Effective implementation requires collaboration among governments, industry actors, and waste management providers to ensure that systems are accessible, efficient, and aligned with broader environmental goals.

Ocean Clean-Up Technologies and Reuse Markets

Ocean clean-up technologies focus on removing existing waste from marine environments while supporting broader circular strategies that prevent future pollution. These technologies range from large-scale systems designed to capture floating debris in offshore areas to small devices used in rivers, ports, and coastal zones. Floating barriers, skimmers, and automated collection platforms are used to intercept plastics before they disperse into open waters. These systems rely on ocean currents, wind patterns, and strategic placement to capture debris efficiently. In ports and marinas, smaller devices such as surface skimmers and suction-based units collect waste from confined areas where pollution tends to accumulate.

River-based clean-up technologies play an important role because a significant share of marine plastic originates from river systems. Interceptors, booms, and filtration devices installed in waterways capture waste before it reaches the ocean. These systems operate continuously and require minimal manual intervention, making them suitable for urban areas with high volumes of waste entering drainage systems. By targeting waste at its source, river clean-up technologies reduce the burden on marine clean-up efforts and improve the efficiency of overall waste management strategies.

Underwater collection systems address debris that settles on the seabed or becomes entangled in habitats. Divers, remotely operated vehicles, and specialized lifting equipment retrieve lost fishing gear, metal debris, and other heavy items. Advances in robotics support deeper and more complex recovery missions, allowing for efficient retrieval without disturbing sensitive habitats. In some regions, community-led underwater clean-ups supplement these technologies, contributing valuable data on debris types and distribution patterns.

Once collected, marine plastics and other recovered materials must be processed in ways that support circularity. Sorting is a critical first step to separate materials based on composition and quality. Clean, high-quality plastics can be mechanically recycled into pellets used for manufacturing new products. Contaminated plastics may require washing, shredding, or chemical recycling processes that break polymers into base components suitable for reuse. Fishing gear made from nylon or polyethylene can often be recycled into textiles, flooring materials, or construction products. Metals recovered from the seabed have established pathways into scrap markets, supporting further circular use.

Chemical recycling technologies expand reuse opportunities for plastics that cannot be processed mechanically. Techniques such as pyrolysis and depolymerization transform mixed or degraded plastics into oils or monomers used in the production of new materials. These processes offer flexibility in handling diverse plastic streams and can help address materials collected from ocean clean-up operations that may be weathered, fragmented, or contaminated. Investment in chemical recycling infrastructure increases the range of materials that can be incorporated into circular markets.

Reuse markets benefit from strong demand for products made from recovered marine materials. Companies are incorporating ocean plastics into consumer goods such as clothing, footwear, bags, and home accessories. These products highlight the environmental narrative behind recovered materials, appealing to consumers seeking sustainable options. Partnerships between clean-up organizations and manufacturers help establish reliable supply chains and support consistent product quality. Transparent certification schemes and labeling standards provide assurance that products contain verified recovered marine materials.

In addition to consumer goods, recovered materials support industrial applications. Recycled plastic can be used in insulation, composite panels, and injection-molded components. Fishing gear recycled into durable polymers finds use in automotive parts, electronics casings, and industrial containers. Expanding industrial reuse markets increases the economic viability of recovery operations and reduces reliance on virgin materials. For metals, established recycling industries help maintain strong markets that support circular use.

Coastal communities play a significant role in developing reuse markets by participating in collection efforts, processing activities, and local manufacturing. Small-scale enterprises can convert recovered materials into artisan products or locally branded goods that support community livelihoods. Training programs and technical support help communities develop skills for sorting, cleaning, and processing recovered materials. These initiatives strengthen local economies and increase support for clean-up activities.

Government policies and international cooperation help enable reuse markets by setting standards, supporting research, and facilitating market development. Incentives such as grants, tax benefits, and procurement policies that favor recycled materials encourage investment in recovery and processing systems. Harmonized regulations across regions support the movement of recovered materials and attract investors to circular supply chains.

Ocean clean-up technologies and reuse markets work together to reduce environmental impacts, recover valuable resources, and advance circularity in marine systems.

Integrating Circularity into Coastal Waste Management Systems

Integrating circularity into coastal waste management systems requires coordinated efforts to reduce waste generation, improve resource recovery, and strengthen infrastructure in communities located near marine environments. Coastal regions face unique challenges due to tourism, fishing activities, maritime transport, and population density, which can place pressure on local waste management services. Circular approaches support the transition from linear disposal practices toward systems that prioritize reuse, recycling, and responsible material flows.

Improving waste collection is foundational to circular coastal systems. Many coastal areas experience fluctuating waste volumes driven by seasonal tourism, making consistent collection difficult. Establishing flexible collection schedules, improving access to waste bins, and providing separate containers for recyclables support better waste segregation. In fishing communities, designated drop-off points for gear, ropes, and nets help prevent waste from entering the ocean. Integrating digital tools to track collection patterns and waste volumes enhances planning and ensures that systems adapt to changing needs.

Recycling infrastructure plays a central role in circular coastal waste management. Coastal municipalities often lack facilities capable of processing a wide range of materials, particularly plastics and mixed waste. Upgrading local recycling centers or establishing partnerships with regional facilities can improve processing capacity. Mobile recycling units and community-driven sorting stations help bridge gaps in areas where permanent infrastructure is not feasible. Clear labeling and public training programs improve the quality of sorted materials, supporting higher recycling rates and reducing contamination that can undermine circular value chains.

Organic waste management is another key component, especially in coastal areas where seafood processing and tourism create substantial amounts of biodegradable waste. Composting facilities, anaerobic digestion plants, and small-scale community composting initiatives convert organic waste into valuable products such as soil amendments and biogas. These systems help reduce landfill use, lower emissions associated with decomposing organic materials, and return nutrients to agricultural and horticultural systems. When coordinated with local businesses, organic waste programs can create reliable supply chains for biomass processing.

Port waste management systems support circularity by providing services that allow vessels to offload waste responsibly. Ports equipped with reception facilities for plastics, oil residues, sewage, and food waste reduce the likelihood of illegal dumping at sea. Improving reception capacity, establishing efficient reporting procedures, and creating incentives for proper waste disposal encourage compliance from maritime operators. Ports can also serve as collection hubs for end-of-life fishing gear and other marine-related waste, enabling recycling and resource recovery at scale.

Informal waste collection systems are common in many coastal regions and can be integrated into circular strategies with appropriate support. Informal collectors often have detailed knowledge of local waste flows and play a significant role in recovering recyclable materials. Providing training, safety equipment, and formal recognition helps improve working conditions while strengthening recycling networks. Integrating informal workers into municipal waste systems expands capacity and supports more accurate waste sorting.

Community engagement is essential for successful circular coastal waste management. Public awareness campaigns can highlight the environmental impacts of marine litter and the importance of proper waste disposal. Programs that involve schools, local organizations, and coastal residents help build a culture of resource responsibility. Citizen science initiatives, such as beach clean-ups and waste audits, generate data on pollution patterns and foster local ownership of circular solutions. Engaging tourism operators helps ensure visitors understand and follow local waste management practices.

Regulation and policy frameworks influence how coastal waste systems incorporate circular principles. Policies that require source separation, set recycling targets, and mandate proper disposal of fishing gear support circular objectives. Local governments can introduce incentives such as reduced waste fees for households and businesses that participate in recycling programs. Integration of circularity into coastal zoning, tourism management plans, and port regulations ensures that waste considerations are embedded in broader development strategies.

Market development for recycled materials is important for maintaining the viability of circular waste systems. Encouraging local industries to use recycled inputs creates stable demand and reduces reliance on external markets. Small businesses in coastal communities can produce value-added products from recovered materials, fostering local economic activity. Partnerships with manufacturers, retailers, and regional distributors help expand these markets and support consistent material flows.

Monitoring and data-driven decision-making strengthen circular coastal waste systems. Tracking waste quantities, composition, and disposal patterns allows authorities to identify gaps and improve efficiency. Environmental monitoring helps detect hotspots of marine litter and assess the effectiveness of interventions. Collaboration among municipalities, research institutions, and industry stakeholders ensures that policies and practices evolve based on evidence.

Integrating circularity into coastal waste management systems requires investments in infrastructure, capacity building, community participation, and supportive policy frameworks. These elements work together to reduce marine pollution and promote more sustainable use of resources in coastal regions.

Chapter 6: Circular Infrastructure and Renewable Energy in the Blue Economy

This chapter examines the role of renewable energy and circular infrastructure design in advancing sustainable marine development. It discusses offshore wind, tidal, and wave energy systems and explores how circular design principles can be applied to ports and coastal structures. The chapter also considers strategies for managing infrastructure throughout its life cycle.

Offshore Wind, Tidal, and Wave Energy Integration

Offshore wind, tidal, and wave energy systems contribute to circularity in the Blue Economy by diversifying renewable energy sources and reducing dependence on fossil fuels. Integrating these energy systems supports decarbonization goals while creating opportunities for efficient use of marine space, improved resource management, and long-term sustainability. Offshore renewable energy technologies operate in dynamic marine environments, and their integration requires careful planning, robust design, and coordination across sectors.

Offshore wind energy is currently the most mature and widely deployed of the marine renewable technologies. Turbines are installed in shallow or deep waters and connected to onshore grids through submarine cables. Advances in turbine design, including larger rotor diameters and floating platforms, allow installations farther from shore where wind speeds are higher and environmental impacts may be reduced. Offshore wind contributes to circularity by providing a low-emission energy source that supports electrification of marine industries and coastal communities. The development of hybrid platforms that combine wind energy with other functions, such as aquaculture facilities or environmental monitoring stations, can optimize marine space use and promote multi-purpose infrastructure.

Tidal energy systems harness predictable tidal currents to generate electricity. These systems rely on turbines placed in areas where tidal flows are strong and consistent, such as narrow channels or estuaries. The predictability of tides provides a stable and reliable energy source that complements variable sources like wind and solar. Tidal technologies include horizontal-axis turbines, vertical-axis turbines, and tidal barrages. Designing these systems for ease of maintenance and component recovery aligns with circular principles by enabling reuse and recycling at the end of operational life. Environmental assessments are essential to ensure that tidal installations do not disrupt sediment transport or marine habitats.

Wave energy systems capture the kinetic energy of surface waves using devices such as point absorbers, oscillating water columns, and attenuators. Wave energy is abundant in many coastal regions and offers a significant resource for future development. Integrating wave energy into the broader renewable energy mix requires addressing challenges related to durability, cost, and grid connection. Advances in materials and engineering help improve resilience to harsh ocean conditions, extending device life and reducing maintenance needs. Designing wave energy devices with modular components allows easier replacement, refurbishment, and repurposing, contributing to circularity.

Co-locating wind, tidal, and wave energy systems enhances the efficiency of marine spatial planning. Shared infrastructure such as cables, substations, and maintenance vessels reduces costs and environmental footprints. Coordinating installations in designated marine energy zones helps limit conflicts with fisheries, shipping, and conservation areas. Multi-use platforms that integrate renewable energy with aquaculture, marine research, or environmental monitoring create opportunities for circular synergies across sectors. These integrated systems support efficient use of resources and help distribute economic benefits among local industries.

Grid integration is a critical factor for scaling offshore renewable energy. Submarine cables, offshore substations, and smart grid technologies are needed to transmit energy to shore and balance supply and demand. Energy storage technologies, such as battery systems or hydrogen production, support the integration of variable energy sources. Hydrogen generated from offshore renewable energy can be used to decarbonize shipping, port operations, and coastal industries, creating circular connections between energy production and end-use sectors. Coordinating grid development with marine energy expansion ensures that infrastructure supports long-term growth and reliability.

Environmental considerations influence the design and deployment of offshore renewable energy. Assessments evaluate potential impacts on marine mammals, fish, seabirds, and benthic habitats. Mitigation measures may include adjusting turbine placement, limiting noise during construction, and implementing monitoring systems. Passive acoustic monitoring and other technologies help track environmental conditions and ensure compliance with regulatory standards. These measures support the integration of renewable energy systems into marine environments without compromising ecological integrity.

Supply chain development is essential for supporting circularity in offshore renewable energy. Sourcing durable, recyclable materials for turbines, cables, and platforms reduces long-term environmental impacts. Establishing regional manufacturing hubs near coastal areas helps reduce transportation emissions and supports local economies. At the end of project life cycles, decommissioning plans emphasize recovering materials, repurposing components, and minimizing waste. Recycling blades, metals, and electronic components contributes to circular value chains.

Collaboration among governments, industry actors, research institutions, and coastal communities supports the successful integration of offshore wind, tidal, and wave energy systems. Policy frameworks that streamline permitting, provide financial incentives, and support research reduce barriers to deployment. Cross-sector partnerships help identify synergies between energy production and other marine activities, contributing to comprehensive and sustainable use of ocean space.

Circular Design of Ports, Platforms, and Coastal Infrastructure

Circular design of ports, platforms, and coastal infrastructure focuses on minimizing resource use, extending asset life cycles, and reducing environmental impacts throughout the design, construction, operation, and decommissioning phases. This approach emphasizes modularity, durability, material recovery, and the integration of renewable energy and resource-efficient technologies. Applying circular principles to coastal and maritime infrastructure supports long-term sustainability while improving the resilience of systems exposed to dynamic marine conditions.

Ports serve as major hubs of economic activity and generate significant material and energy demands. Circular design in ports begins with selecting durable, low-impact materials that can withstand marine environments while remaining recyclable at the end of their service life. Concrete alternatives, corrosion-resistant metals, and bio-based composites extend infrastructure longevity. Modularity allows port components such as quays, cranes, and storage facilities to be repaired, upgraded, or replaced without dismantling entire structures. This reduces waste and lowers the cost of maintaining critical infrastructure. Incorporating renewable energy systems such as rooftop solar, on-site wind, or access to offshore renewable energy supports decarbonization and reduces reliance on fossil fuels in port operations.

Operational efficiency within ports is central to circularity. Shore power systems allow vessels to shut down engines while docked, reducing emissions and lowering noise pollution. Digital platforms optimize cargo handling, route planning, and vessel scheduling, reducing fuel use and improving turnaround times. Water recycling systems treat wastewater generated by port activities for reuse in cleaning, cooling, or irrigation. Waste reception facilities enable proper disposal and segregation of materials from vessels, fishing fleets, and port operations. Integrating recycling centers within port complexes strengthens the capacity to process recovered materials and return them to supply chains.

Circular design principles also apply to offshore platforms used for energy production, research, or aquaculture. Designing platforms for ease of maintenance and disassembly ensures that components can be reused or recycled at the end of their operational life. Floating structures benefit from modular construction, enabling sections to be detached, repaired, or upgraded individually. Using materials that are recyclable, durable, and resistant to marine corrosion reduces lifecycle impacts. Platforms can be co-located or integrated with multiple functions, such as combining renewable energy generation with aquaculture systems or environmental monitoring stations, improving resource efficiency and maximizing use of marine space.

Nature-based solutions complement circular infrastructure by enhancing ecological performance while supporting engineering objectives. Coastal protection structures can incorporate living shorelines, restored wetlands, mangroves, or oyster reefs to reduce erosion, buffer storm impacts, and improve water quality. Hybrid designs that combine natural and built elements reduce maintenance costs and support biodiversity. Breakwaters and revetments designed with ecological enhancements provide habitats for marine life while maintaining structural integrity. These solutions contribute to regenerative outcomes that align with circularity by restoring ecosystems affected by development.

Circular approaches influence the design and management of coastal facilities such as terminals, marinas, and waterfront developments. Using permeable surfaces, water-efficient landscaping, and stormwater capture systems reduces runoff and minimizes impacts on nearshore ecosystems. Buildings can incorporate low-carbon materials, passive cooling strategies, and renewable energy technologies. Designing facilities for adaptability allows them to respond to changing sea levels, climate conditions, or operational needs without requiring full reconstruction. This reduces material use, cost, and environmental disturbance over time.

Decommissioning and repurposing play important roles in circular coastal infrastructure. As ports, platforms, and coastal facilities age, planning for end-of-life scenarios ensures that materials are recovered, reused, or recycled. Metals, electrical components, and structural materials can be processed and reintegrated into new construction projects. Some decommissioned structures, particularly offshore platforms, may be repurposed for artificial reefs, research installations, or renewable energy foundations if ecological and safety assessments support such transitions. Repurposing reduces waste and preserves the embodied energy in existing structures.

Digitalization supports circular design by enabling predictive maintenance, resource monitoring, and lifecycle management. Sensors embedded in infrastructure track structural health, corrosion, and performance conditions, enabling timely repairs that extend asset life. Data analytics support better planning, reducing downtime and minimizing material replacements. Lifecycle assessment tools help designers evaluate the environmental impacts of materials and construction methods, guiding decisions that favor circularity.

Governance frameworks influence the extent to which circular design principles are adopted in ports, offshore platforms, and coastal infrastructure. Regulations that encourage material reuse, mandate environmental performance standards, or incentivize renewable energy integration support circular objectives. Collaboration among engineers, planners, industry operators, and environmental organizations ensures that infrastructure development aligns with community needs and ecological considerations.

End-of-Life Management of Marine Renewable Infrastructure

End-of-life management of marine renewable infrastructure is an essential component of circular approaches in the offshore energy sector. As offshore wind, tidal, and wave energy installations expand, the need for responsible decommissioning strategies grows. These strategies ensure that materials are recovered, reused, or recycled rather than becoming marine debris or occupying valuable ocean space. Effective management requires comprehensive planning from the earliest stages of project development and coordination among regulators, operators, and supply chain actors.

Planning for end-of-life begins with designing infrastructure that can be dismantled efficiently. Modular construction, standardized components, and the use of durable, recyclable materials support easier disassembly and reduce waste generation. Developers integrate decommissioning considerations into initial project designs, selecting materials that withstand marine conditions while remaining suitable for recovery. Turbine towers, foundations, cables, and mechanical components are predominantly made from metals that can be recycled. Early planning also includes offshore surveys to identify site conditions that may influence decommissioning methods.

During decommissioning, infrastructure is typically removed in stages to minimize environmental disturbance. Turbines are dismantled piece by piece, often using specialized vessels equipped with lifting cranes. Components such as blades, nacelles, and towers are transported to shore for processing. Foundations may be removed entirely or partially, depending on regulatory requirements and ecological assessments. In some cases, partial removal is preferred when complete extraction could damage sensitive marine habitats. Subsea cables are either recovered for recycling or left in place if removal presents environmental risks.

Recycling plays a central role in end-of-life management. Metals such as steel, copper, and aluminum from turbines and substations have established recycling pathways that support their reintroduction into industrial supply chains. These materials retain high value and can be repurposed with minimal quality loss. The recycling of composite materials, particularly turbine blades, presents greater challenges. Blades are typically made from fiberglass or carbon fiber composites that require specialized processes for recovery. Emerging technologies such as mechanical grinding, pyrolysis, and chemical recycling offer potential pathways for handling composite waste. Research continues to improve the efficiency and cost-effectiveness of these methods, enabling higher recovery rates.

Alternative uses for decommissioned components can extend the lifespan of materials and reduce the need for recycling. Blades have been repurposed into pedestrian bridges, sound barriers, playground structures, and architectural elements. These applications preserve the embodied energy in composite materials and reduce the environmental impact associated with producing new construction materials. Offshore foundations and platforms may be repurposed for artificial reefs, aquaculture installations, or research stations when ecological and safety assessments support such conversions. Repurposing reduces waste and enhances the multifunctionality of marine infrastructure.

Environmental considerations guide decisions throughout the decommissioning process. Assessments evaluate potential impacts on marine species, benthic habitats, water quality, and sediment dynamics. Timing decommissioning activities to avoid sensitive periods for marine life, such as breeding or migration, helps minimize disturbance. Noise mitigation measures and careful management of debris prevent harm to marine mammals and fish populations. Sediment management strategies address the potential release of buried materials or contaminants during cable recovery.

Regulatory frameworks shape end-of-life management practices by defining responsibilities, performance standards, and reporting requirements. Many jurisdictions require developers to submit decommissioning plans as part of project approval processes. These plans outline timelines, removal methods, waste management strategies, and site restoration measures. Bonds or financial assurances may be required to ensure that decommissioning obligations are fulfilled even if project operators change or cease operations. Harmonizing regulations across regions supports consistent practices and facilitates cross-border cooperation.

Logistics and supply chain coordination are critical for carrying out decommissioning activities efficiently. Decommissioning requires specialized vessels, trained personnel, and onshore facilities capable of handling large components. Ports play an important role as hubs for receiving, dismantling, and sorting materials. Expanding port infrastructure to accommodate decommissioning operations enhances regional capacity and supports emerging circular industries. Collaboration with recycling companies, manufacturers, and material processors ensures that recovered materials enter appropriate value chains.

Data collection throughout the operational life of infrastructure supports better end-of-life planning. Monitoring information on structural integrity, material degradation, and environmental performance helps operators anticipate decommissioning needs and select appropriate methods. Digital records of component materials and maintenance histories facilitate sorting for recycling or repurposing. Integrating decommissioning data into lifecycle assessments supports broader efforts to reduce environmental impacts across renewable energy supply chains.

End-of-life management for marine renewable infrastructure requires integrated approaches that combine design, policy, technology, and environmental stewardship. Through responsible dismantling, material recovery, and repurposing, these practices contribute to circularity in the offshore energy sector and support sustainable use of marine resources.

Resource Efficiency in Maritime Construction

Resource efficiency in maritime construction focuses on minimizing material use, reducing waste, and optimizing processes throughout the lifecycle of coastal and offshore infrastructure. This approach supports circularity by encouraging the use of durable materials, promoting modular construction methods, and enhancing the reuse and recycling of components. Maritime construction encompasses ports, seawalls, offshore platforms, renewable energy installations, and related structures, all of which benefit from resource-efficient strategies that extend asset lifespan and lower environmental impacts.

Material selection is central to resource-efficient construction. Choosing materials that are durable, corrosion-resistant, and recyclable reduces long-term resource consumption and maintenance needs. High-performance concretes, fiber-reinforced polymers, and advanced steel alloys extend structural life in harsh marine environments. Using low-carbon cement alternatives, recycled aggregates, and bio-based materials helps lower the environmental footprint of construction projects. Material passports, which document the composition and characteristics of construction materials, support future recovery and recycling by improving traceability.

Modular design improves efficiency by allowing components to be prefabricated offsite and assembled quickly in marine environments. Prefabrication reduces construction time, lowers energy use, and enhances quality control by manufacturing components in controlled settings. Modular structures can be easily repaired, upgraded, or replaced without demolishing entire facilities. This flexibility reduces waste generation and supports adaptive reuse as operational needs change. For offshore infrastructure, modular platforms and turbine components simplify installation and decommissioning processes, supporting circularity throughout project lifecycles.

Construction processes influence the degree of resource efficiency achieved. Digital tools such as building information modeling support precise planning of material quantities, reducing overordering and minimizing waste. These tools help project teams simulate structural performance, optimize designs, and identify opportunities for efficiency. Automation in cutting, welding, and assembly improves accuracy and reduces material loss. Transport efficiency is enhanced by optimizing logistics and using vessels with lower fuel consumption or hybrid propulsion systems, reducing emissions during construction activities.

Waste reduction and recycling practices are essential components of resource-efficient maritime construction. Construction sites generate waste from packaging, offcuts, excavation, and demolition. Implementing onsite sorting and recycling systems helps divert materials from landfills, especially metals, aggregates, and plastics. Recycled aggregates from demolition can be reused in new construction, reducing the need for virgin resources. In coastal protection projects, natural materials such as rocks, timber, or biodegradable structures can be reused or returned to ecological functions when decommissioned. Establishing partnerships with recycling facilities improves material recovery rates and supports local circular economies.

Energy efficiency contributes to resource-efficient construction by lowering the operational impacts of building and maintaining maritime infrastructure. Using renewable energy sources during construction, such as temporary solar or wind systems, reduces reliance on fuel-powered generators. Selecting equipment with high energy performance and reducing idle times on construction sites further decreases energy use. Integrating energy-efficient technologies into the final design, including LED lighting, advanced cooling systems, and renewable energy connections, enhances long-term sustainability.

Ecological considerations guide construction techniques that reduce disruption to marine habitats and support resource efficiency. Minimizing dredging, avoiding critical habitats, and using low-impact installation methods protect ecosystems and maintain natural coastal functions. Nature-based construction materials, such as engineered reefs or bio-enhancing additives in concrete, promote biodiversity while providing structural stability. These approaches reduce the need for additional protective measures and contribute to long-term resilience.

Lifecycle planning strengthens resource efficiency by considering the full span of construction, operation, maintenance, and decommissioning. Designing infrastructure for extended service life reduces the frequency of major repairs or replacements. Scheduled maintenance prevents premature failure and preserves material integrity. When infrastructure reaches the end of its operational life, planning for disassembly and material recovery helps ensure that valuable resources re-enter supply chains. Lifecycle assessments help project teams evaluate environmental impacts and identify improvements that support circularity.

Collaboration among engineers, architects, contractors, regulators, and local communities supports resource-efficient construction through shared knowledge and coordinated planning. Regulations that encourage recycled content, mandate waste management plans, or incentivize energy-efficient practices promote the adoption of resource-efficient methods. Procurement policies that prioritize sustainable materials and circular design strengthen market demand for resource-efficient products and services.

Resource efficiency in maritime construction contributes to sustainable development by reducing environmental impacts, supporting resilient infrastructure, and promoting circular use of materials.

Chapter 7: Finance and Investment in Circular Blue Economy Models

This chapter outlines financial mechanisms that support circular approaches in marine sectors. It examines instruments such as blue bonds, blended finance, and impact investment, highlighting how they can mobilize capital for sustainable initiatives. The chapter discusses the importance of de-risking and aligning investment with environmental and social objectives.

Sustainable Blue Finance Instruments

Sustainable blue finance instruments support the transition toward a circular and regenerative Blue Economy by directing capital toward projects that protect marine ecosystems, promote sustainable resource use, and reduce environmental impacts. These instruments provide structured financial mechanisms that help governments, businesses, and communities invest in sustainable ocean-related activities. They also create incentives for aligning economic development with ecological stewardship, ensuring that marine resources are managed responsibly over the long term.

Blue bonds have emerged as a prominent financial instrument dedicated to ocean-related sustainability goals. Issued by governments, development banks, or corporations, blue bonds raise capital for projects such as marine conservation, wastewater treatment, sustainable fisheries, and coastal resilience infrastructure. These bonds operate similarly to green bonds but are explicitly tied to ocean health outcomes. Blue bond frameworks typically include clear eligibility criteria, monitoring requirements, and reporting standards to ensure transparency and accountability. Investors support these instruments because they offer stable returns while contributing to environmental objectives.

Sustainability-linked bonds represent another category of blue finance instruments. Rather than funding specific projects, these bonds tie interest rates or financial terms to the issuer's performance against predefined sustainability targets. In marine sectors, these targets may include reducing pollution, improving energy efficiency, or achieving certification for sustainable practices. If the issuer fails to meet the targets, financial penalties apply. Sustainability-linked bonds encourage companies to embed sustainability into core operations and track their progress through measurable indicators.

Blue loans function similarly to blue bonds but are issued through banking institutions rather than capital markets. These loans support projects that align with sustainable ocean priorities, including renewable energy installations, circular aquaculture systems, port upgrades, and marine habitat restoration. Concessional loans, which offer favorable terms such as lower interest rates or extended repayment periods, play an important role in financing early-stage circular innovations. By reducing financial barriers, these instruments help scale technologies and practices that may not yet be fully commercialized.

Blended finance is a mechanism that combines public, private, and philanthropic capital to reduce investment risks and attract private sector participation in blue economy initiatives. Public or philanthropic funds absorb some of the financial risks associated with complex or innovative projects, making them more attractive to commercial investors. Blended finance structures can support wastewater treatment upgrades, coastal resilience measures, or community-based conservation. They create opportunities for collaboration among governments, development agencies, impact investors, and private companies.

Guarantees and insurance products also support sustainable blue finance by mitigating risks related to environmental uncertainties, regulatory conditions, or long-term project viability. Partial risk guarantees can encourage investment in emerging technologies such as wave or tidal energy by covering specific project risks that investors may be unwilling to assume. Insurance mechanisms protect assets vulnerable to climate-related hazards such as storms, erosion, or sea-level rise. These financial tools help stabilize project financing and support resilience in marine sectors.

Impact investment funds dedicated to the Blue Economy provide another avenue for sustainable financing. These funds invest in companies or initiatives that demonstrate measurable environmental and social benefits alongside financial returns. Impact funds may support ventures in sustainable aquaculture, marine biotechnology, circular waste management, and renewable energy. By prioritizing both environmental performance and profitability, these funds help expand markets for circular and restorative marine activities.

Public finance institutions, including multilateral development banks, play a key role in providing technical assistance, concessional funding, and capacity-building support. Their involvement often signals credibility and reduces risks for private investors. Development banks may also support the creation of national blue finance frameworks, improve regulatory environments, and facilitate regional coordination. Technical assistance initiatives help governments develop project pipelines, strengthen monitoring systems, and implement best practices.

Policy frameworks influence the effectiveness of blue finance instruments by establishing clear regulatory conditions, environmental standards, and reporting requirements. National blue economy strategies, marine spatial plans, and climate policies help align financial flows with long-term sustainability goals. Incentives such as tax benefits, subsidies for clean technologies, and regulatory reforms that promote circularity enhance the attractiveness of blue finance instruments.

Transparency and accountability mechanisms ensure that funds raised through blue finance instruments are used effectively. Monitoring systems track environmental outcomes such as reduced pollution, improved water quality, or increased biodiversity. Reporting standards and third-party verification help maintain investor confidence and demonstrate progress toward sustainability commitments. These systems support continual improvement and encourage broader adoption of blue finance instruments across marine sectors.

Sustainable blue finance instruments create pathways for mobilizing capital toward initiatives that foster healthy oceans, resilient coastal communities, and circular economic systems.

ESG Criteria, Impact Investors, and Investment Standards

Environmental, social, and governance criteria play an important role in directing investment toward sustainable and responsible practices in the Blue Economy. ESG frameworks allow investors to evaluate how organizations manage environmental impacts, engage with communities, and govern their operations. In marine sectors, this includes assessing how companies address pollution, resource use, labor conditions, and regulatory compliance. ESG criteria help identify risks associated with unsustainable practices and highlight opportunities for businesses that adopt circular and regenerative approaches. These assessments increasingly influence investment decisions as markets recognize the importance of aligning financial performance with environmental stewardship.

Environmental criteria are central to evaluating marine-related activities. These criteria examine issues such as greenhouse gas emissions, waste management, biodiversity impacts, and the sustainable use of marine resources. Companies operating in fisheries, aquaculture, shipping, and offshore energy must demonstrate effective strategies for reducing environmental pressures. This may include adopting cleaner technologies, improving efficiency, enhancing traceability, or integrating circular solutions such as waste recovery and resource reuse. Environmental indicators also consider how organizations adapt to climate risks, including sea-level rise, extreme weather events, and shifting species distributions.

Social criteria assess how companies interact with workers, communities, and consumers. In the Blue Economy, this includes ensuring fair labor practices in fishing and seafood processing, promoting safety in offshore operations, and respecting the rights of Indigenous and coastal communities. Social performance also involves contributing to local livelihoods, supporting capacity building, and fostering inclusive economic development. Companies that engage constructively with communities and prioritize equitable outcomes are more likely to attract impact-oriented investment. Social criteria further consider how businesses contribute to food security, public health, and cultural values tied to marine environments.

Governance criteria focus on corporate transparency, ethical behavior, regulatory compliance, and accountability. Strong governance frameworks support informed decision-making and reduce risks associated with corruption, regulatory violations, or mismanagement. For marine industries, governance considerations include adherence to maritime safety standards, compliance with fishing regulations, and responsible oversight of environmental impacts. Transparent reporting and stakeholder engagement help build trust with investors and regulators. Governance standards also assess the extent to which sustainability objectives are embedded within corporate strategies and overseen by leadership.

Impact investors play a significant role in accelerating sustainable development in the Blue Economy. These investors seek measurable environmental and social outcomes alongside financial returns. Their involvement supports projects such as sustainable aquaculture, marine conservation, waste reduction, and renewable energy integration. Impact investors often focus on early-stage innovations and community-based initiatives that may struggle to attract traditional financing. They use tools such as impact measurement frameworks, performance indicators, and third-party verification to track progress and ensure accountability. By prioritizing long-term value over short-term gains, impact investors help scale circular solutions.

Investment standards guide the integration of ESG criteria and impact objectives into financial decision-making. International frameworks such as the Principles for Responsible Investment and the Equator Principles provide guidelines for incorporating environmental and social considerations into lending and investment practices. Sector-specific standards, including those for sustainable seafood, shipping decarbonization, and marine renewable energy, help refine expectations for different industries. These standards encourage consistency across markets and reduce uncertainty for investors seeking responsible investment opportunities.

Certification schemes play an important role in demonstrating compliance with sustainability standards. Certifications for sustainable fisheries, organic aquaculture, and responsible marine tourism provide assurances that a company's operations meet defined criteria. These certifications often require third-party audits and continuous improvement processes. Certification signals to investors that a company is committed to responsible practices and adheres to recognized standards. Similarly, sustainability-linked financing instruments use performance metrics tied to specific standards to evaluate progress.

Reporting frameworks support transparency and allow investors to assess environmental and social performance. Companies use sustainability reports, impact statements, and disclosure platforms to communicate progress toward ESG goals. International frameworks such as the Global Reporting Initiative and the Task Force on Climate-related Financial Disclosures provide templates for consistent reporting. These frameworks help companies disclose climate risks, governance structures, and mitigation strategies. Transparent reporting supports investor confidence and enables better alignment between capital flows and sustainability objectives.

Regulatory developments strengthen the integration of ESG criteria into marine investment. Governments increasingly require disclosure of environmental and climate-related risks, particularly for large companies and financial institutions. Regulations may also set minimum sustainability performance requirements for certain activities, such as aquaculture licensing or port development. These measures create incentives for companies to adopt responsible practices and encourage investors to prioritize sustainable investments.

Collaboration among financial institutions, regulators, industry groups, and civil society enhances the development and application of ESG criteria and investment standards. Joint initiatives help harmonize metrics, improve data quality, and support knowledge exchange. Through collective efforts, these actors contribute to a financial ecosystem that rewards sustainability and encourages circular and regenerative practices across the Blue Economy.

Scaling Innovation via Public-Private Partnerships

Public-private partnerships support the scaling of circular and sustainable innovations in the Blue Economy by combining the strengths of governments, private companies, research institutions, and civil society. These partnerships enable investment in infrastructure, technology development, and capacity building that might not be achievable through public or private actors alone. Through shared responsibilities, risk allocation, and collaborative planning, public-private partnerships help accelerate the deployment of solutions that promote resource efficiency, environmental protection, and long-term economic development.

One of the key advantages of public-private partnerships is their ability to mobilize diverse financial resources. Governments can provide grants, concessional loans, or guarantees that reduce financial risks for private investors. Private companies contribute capital, technical expertise, and operational capacity. Development banks and philanthropic organizations may also participate to bridge funding gaps or support early-stage innovations. This combination of resources enables the scaling of projects such as marine renewable energy installations, circular aquaculture systems, coastal resilience infrastructure, and waste management facilities.

Innovation benefits from public-private partnerships through coordinated research and development. Governments and research institutions can generate scientific knowledge and pilot new technologies, while private companies help commercialize and deploy solutions at scale. Joint research programs support innovations such as biodegradable fishing gear, advanced water treatment technologies, energy-efficient vessel designs, and digital monitoring tools. Pilot projects allow stakeholders to test circular solutions in real-world conditions, refine methodologies, and identify pathways for wider adoption. Partnerships ensure that technological advancements are grounded in practical applications and aligned with regulatory frameworks.

Public-private partnerships also strengthen policy development by creating platforms for dialogue between regulators and industry actors. These interactions help policymakers understand technological trends, operational challenges, and investment barriers. In turn, companies gain clarity on regulatory expectations and environmental standards. Collaborative policy design supports the development of effective marine spatial plans, sustainable fisheries regulations, port management strategies, and circular waste management systems. Clear and supportive regulatory environments reduce uncertainty and encourage private-sector investment in sustainable initiatives.

Infrastructure development is a major area where public-private partnerships contribute to circularity. Projects such as port upgrades, renewable energy installations, and waste reception facilities require significant investment and long-term coordination. Partnerships enable shared responsibility for construction, operation, and maintenance. For example, a port authority may work with private operators to build recycling centers, digitized logistics systems, or energy-efficient terminal facilities. Offshore renewable energy projects often involve public-private collaboration to develop transmission lines, grid connections, and environmental monitoring programs.

Community engagement is enhanced through public-private partnerships, ensuring that local needs and knowledge inform project design. Coastal communities, Indigenous groups, and small-scale fishers can participate in planning processes, providing insights into environmental conditions, social priorities, and cultural values. Partnerships that include community actors support the development of inclusive projects such as community-based aquaculture, eco-tourism initiatives, and local recycling enterprises. Engagement helps build trust, improves project outcomes, and strengthens social license to operate.

In the fisheries and aquaculture sectors, public-private partnerships help advance traceability, data collection, and sustainable certification. Governments may collaborate with technology companies to develop digital systems that track catch data, monitor vessel activity, or assess environmental performance. Private companies implement these systems across supply chains, improving transparency and meeting market demands for sustainable products. Joint initiatives also support training programs for fishers, processors, and coastal workers, strengthening capacity for adopting circular practices.

Environmental monitoring and conservation efforts benefit from partnerships that combine scientific expertise with private-sector investment. Companies involved in marine industries may support research programs on habitat restoration, species protection, or pollution reduction. Governments can facilitate access to marine areas, coordinate data-sharing, and integrate findings into policy. Partnerships enable long-term monitoring programs that track ecosystem health, assess project impacts, and support adaptive management strategies.

Public-private partnerships also help scale digital innovation in the Blue Economy. Collaborations support the development of data platforms that integrate information from satellites, sensors, autonomous vessels, and environmental databases. These tools enhance resource management, improve operational efficiency, and support decision-making. Digital innovation strengthens circularity by optimizing resource flows, reducing waste, and enabling predictive maintenance of infrastructure.

Barriers to effective partnerships include misaligned priorities, complex governance structures, and financial risks. Clear agreements, transparent communication, and well-defined roles help address these challenges. Standardized partnership models and international guidelines support the development of effective arrangements. Successful partnerships often include mechanisms for conflict resolution, performance monitoring, and accountability.

Scaling innovation through public-private partnerships relies on coordinated action, shared vision, and long-term commitment. These collaborations support the advancement of circular and sustainable solutions across marine sectors and contribute to resilient and regenerative ocean economies.

De-Risking Mechanisms and Enabling Policy Environments

De-risking mechanisms and enabling policy environments support investment in circular and sustainable Blue Economy activities by reducing financial uncertainty, improving regulatory clarity, and creating conditions that encourage private-sector participation. These tools address challenges associated with emerging technologies, long project lifecycles, and environmental variability, making it easier for investors to commit capital to marine and coastal initiatives.

Financial de-risking mechanisms help lower the perceived and actual risks associated with sustainable ocean projects. Guarantees provided by governments or development banks protect investors against specific risks such as project delays, default, or regulatory changes. These guarantees can cover a portion of losses, making investments more attractive to commercial lenders. Insurance products also play a role in de-risking by protecting against natural hazards, equipment failure, or operational disruptions common in marine environments. For offshore renewable energy projects, for example, insurance coverage can help manage risks related to storms, wave impacts, and underwater cable damage.

Concessional finance is another key de-risking mechanism. Development banks, climate funds, and philanthropic organizations offer loans with favorable terms, such as low interest rates or extended repayment periods, to projects that deliver environmental and social benefits. Concessional finance can be blended with private investment to create more balanced risk profiles. This approach is particularly important for early-stage technologies such as wave energy or advanced aquaculture systems, where commercial viability is still developing.

Equity participation by public institutions also reduces risk for private investors. When governments or multilateral institutions invest alongside private companies, it signals confidence in the project's feasibility and long-term potential. Public equity participation can help attract additional investors, accelerate project timelines, and support innovations that require significant upfront capital. This mechanism is frequently used in large-scale infrastructure projects, including port modernization and marine renewable energy.

Credit enhancement tools strengthen the financial profile of projects seeking private funding. These tools may include subordinated debt, which absorbs early losses before senior lenders are affected, or performance-based incentives that reward projects for achieving specific sustainability outcomes. Credit enhancement helps projects secure financing at lower costs and gain access to a broader pool of investors.

Enabling policy environments complement financial de-risking by establishing regulatory stability, clear guidelines, and supportive frameworks. Long-term marine spatial plans guide the allocation of ocean space for activities such as renewable energy, aquaculture, conservation, and shipping. By clarifying where activities can occur, spatial plans reduce conflicts and improve predictability for investors. Policies that streamline permitting processes and reduce administrative delays further support project development.

Environmental regulations and performance standards contribute to de-risking by creating consistent expectations across industries. Clear requirements for waste management, emissions reduction, and habitat protection reduce uncertainty and encourage companies to adopt circular practices. Certification schemes and sustainability labels also help standardize expectations and create market recognition for responsible operations.

Fiscal incentives such as tax credits, accelerated depreciation, and import duty exemptions lower the cost of adopting circular technologies. These incentives can apply to energy-efficient equipment, waste treatment systems, or recycling technologies. Governments may also offer grants for research and development, supporting innovation in areas such as biodegradable materials, advanced monitoring systems, and low-impact infrastructure.

Public procurement policies encourage circularity by prioritizing sustainable products and services in government purchasing decisions. Maritime infrastructure projects that require recycled materials, energy-efficient systems, or nature-based solutions create new markets and signal long-term demand. Procurement policies can be particularly influential in sectors such as port construction, coastal protection, and public aquaculture facilities.

Capacity building and technical assistance strengthen the effectiveness of policy environments by improving the skills and knowledge of stakeholders. Training programs for regulators, investors, and industry operators support the implementation of circular technologies and sustainable practices. Technical assistance for project preparation helps stakeholders develop bankable proposals, conduct feasibility studies, and design monitoring systems.

Cooperation across government agencies, industry groups, and financial institutions ensures that de-risking mechanisms and enabling policies work together effectively. Aligning objectives and coordinating implementation improves outcomes and supports the scaling of circular solutions across marine and coastal sectors.

Chapter 8: Innovation, Technology, and Digitalization for Circularity

This chapter explores how digital tools and technological innovation enable circularity in the blue economy. It examines the role of AI, blockchain, IoT, and marine biotechnology in improving efficiency, transparency, and resource management. The chapter highlights both opportunities and challenges associated with digital transformation.

AI, Blockchain, IoT, and Digital Twins for Marine Resource Management

AI, blockchain, IoT, and digital twin technologies contribute to more efficient, transparent, and adaptive marine resource management. These tools support circularity by improving monitoring, optimizing resource use, reducing waste, and enabling data-driven decision-making across sectors such as fisheries, aquaculture, shipping, and marine conservation. Their integration strengthens the capacity of governments, industries, and communities to manage ocean resources sustainably.

AI plays a central role in analyzing complex datasets generated in marine environments. Machine learning models process information from satellites, sensors, and onboard equipment to identify patterns and generate predictive insights. In fisheries, AI supports stock assessments, vessel tracking, and species identification by analyzing imagery and acoustic data. These applications enhance accuracy and reduce the time required for data processing. In aquaculture, AI-enabled monitoring systems assess fish behavior, feeding efficiency, and water quality, helping operators adjust conditions to reduce waste and improve productivity. AI-based forecasting tools provide early warnings for harmful algal blooms, disease outbreaks, and extreme weather events, improving preparedness.

IoT technologies enable real-time data collection from distributed networks of sensors placed on vessels, aquaculture cages, buoys, and marine infrastructure. These sensors measure parameters such as temperature, salinity, oxygen levels, pH, and current speed. Continuous data flow allows operators to respond quickly to environmental changes, maintain optimal conditions, and reduce resource use. In ports, IoT systems monitor equipment performance, energy use, and logistics processes to enhance operational efficiency. IoT-enabled traceability systems track seafood products from harvest to market, supporting transparency and compliance with sustainability standards.

Blockchain technology strengthens trust and accountability in marine supply chains by providing secure, immutable records of transactions and activities. Blockchain systems can store data related to catch origin, handling practices, certifications, and regulatory compliance. This information is accessible to regulators, companies, and consumers, reducing opportunities for fraud or illegal fishing. Smart contracts automate compliance by executing predefined actions when specific conditions are met, such as verifying sustainability certifications before shipment. In aquaculture, blockchain supports quality assurance by ensuring that feed inputs, stocking densities, and environmental conditions meet regulatory and market requirements.

Digital twins replicate physical marine systems in virtual environments, allowing stakeholders to model scenarios, test interventions, and evaluate performance under different conditions. In aquaculture, digital twins simulate fish growth, water flows, feeding patterns, and infrastructure behavior. These simulations help operators optimize feeding strategies, reduce waste, and plan maintenance activities. Digital twins of offshore energy systems model the performance of turbines, cables, and platforms, supporting predictive maintenance and reducing downtime. In coastal management, digital twins of harbors or marine protected areas help planners evaluate the impacts of development, climate change, or restoration projects.

Integrating these technologies enhances collaboration among stakeholders. Shared data platforms allow governments, scientists, and industry actors to access and analyze information collectively. This supports coordinated management of fisheries, ports, and marine protected areas. Cross-sector data sharing facilitates cumulative impact assessments and improves understanding of ecosystem dynamics. Interoperable systems ensure that data from AI, IoT, blockchain, and digital twins can be combined to support comprehensive decision-making.

These technologies also support enforcement and compliance. AI-enabled vessel monitoring systems detect suspicious activity, such as unauthorized fishing or deviations from approved routes. IoT sensors can verify gear deployment, catch volumes, or environmental conditions in real time. Blockchain-backed documentation ensures that products meet regulatory requirements before entering markets. Digital twins help authorities simulate enforcement strategies and assess their effectiveness.

Challenges associated with adopting these technologies include cost, technical capacity, and data governance. High initial investments may limit access for small-scale fishers, coastal communities, or developing countries. Capacity-building programs help address skill gaps by providing training in data interpretation, equipment maintenance, and digital literacy. Data governance frameworks ensure that information is managed securely, shared responsibly, and used ethically. These frameworks address issues such as data ownership, privacy, interoperability, and equitable access.

Partnerships among governments, technology companies, research institutions, and local communities support broader adoption of these tools. Pilot projects demonstrate practical applications, refine models, and build trust. Public funding and private investment help expand digital infrastructure in remote or underserved regions. Regulatory support ensures that technological innovations align with environmental and social objectives.

AI, blockchain, IoT, and digital twins provide powerful tools for improving efficiency, transparency, and adaptability in marine resource management. Their integration strengthens circular practices by enabling better monitoring, optimizing resource use, and supporting sustainable decision-making across marine sectors.

Smart Fishing, Observation Networks, and Waste Monitoring

Smart fishing technologies, observation networks, and waste monitoring systems contribute to more sustainable and circular practices in marine environments by improving data collection, enhancing decision-making, and reducing the ecological impacts of fishing and waste discharge. These tools help fisheries optimize operations, strengthen compliance, and protect marine ecosystems while supporting long-term resource availability. When combined with broader digital and policy frameworks, they support more adaptive and transparent management of ocean activities.

Smart fishing technologies are designed to increase efficiency while reducing bycatch, minimizing fuel use, and improving stock assessments. Electronic monitoring systems use cameras, sensors, and GPS to document fishing activity, providing accurate data on catch composition, fishing effort, and gear performance. These systems help verify compliance with regulations and contribute to more precise quota management. Smart gear innovations such as illuminated nets, acoustic deterrents, and selective trawl designs reduce the capture of non-target species and support healthier fish stocks. Real-time satellite data and digital mapping tools allow fishers to identify areas with high target-species abundance while avoiding sensitive habitats or restricted zones.

Digital tools that support route optimization help reduce fuel consumption and emissions by identifying the most efficient travel paths based on weather, currents, and sea conditions. Improved navigation technologies reduce the risk of gear loss, which contributes to marine litter and ongoing ecological impacts. Gear-tracking devices using GPS or radio-frequency identification help locate lost equipment, enabling faster retrieval and reducing the accumulation of ghost gear in marine environments.

Observation networks strengthen marine resource management by providing continuous and coordinated environmental monitoring. These networks consist of buoys, underwater sensors, gliders, satellites, and autonomous vehicles that collect data on ocean temperature, salinity, currents, chemistry, and biological activity. This information supports ecosystem-based management by revealing trends in species distribution, habitat conditions, and climate-driven changes. Fisheries scientists use observation data to improve stock assessments, refine models, and guide adaptive management strategies. Observation networks also support early-warning systems for harmful algal blooms, coral bleaching events, or extreme weather conditions.

Collaboration is essential for effective observation networks. National agencies, research institutions, industry groups, and community organizations often share sensors, data platforms, and communication systems. Global and regional networks such as ocean observing systems integrate data from multiple countries to create comprehensive assessments of ocean health. Shared data standards and open-access platforms improve interoperability and allow managers and researchers to use information from diverse sources. This collaborative approach supports more coordinated responses to environmental challenges.

Waste monitoring systems address growing concerns about marine litter, wastewater, and pollution from maritime activities. Digital monitoring tools track waste generation, collection, and disposal at ports, docks, and coastal facilities. Sensors installed in storm drains, river mouths, and coastal areas detect debris movement and help identify pollution hotspots. This information can be used to target interventions, improve waste infrastructure, and evaluate the effectiveness of policies such as bans on single-use plastics or gear disposal regulations.

Remote sensing technologies, including satellite imagery and drones, help track floating debris in offshore and nearshore environments. These tools support clean-up efforts by identifying accumulation zones and monitoring debris movement over time. Waste monitoring systems can also track chemical pollutants such as oil, microplastics, and nutrient runoff. Automated sensors measure water quality indicators and transmit data in real time to coastal managers, who can respond quickly to emerging issues.

In fisheries and aquaculture, waste monitoring technologies help track organic waste, feed inputs, and nutrient flows. Automated feeders, water-quality sensors, and sediment monitors provide insights into waste production and environmental impacts. This information supports management decisions that reduce nutrient pollution, improve feed efficiency, and maintain ecosystem balance. Integrating waste monitoring into regulatory frameworks helps ensure compliance with environmental standards and supports more sustainable production practices.

Community involvement strengthens smart fishing, observation networks, and waste monitoring systems. Fisher-led monitoring programs empower small-scale operators to participate in data collection and resource stewardship. Citizen science initiatives contribute valuable information on coastal litter, species sightings, and water quality. Local communities often have detailed knowledge of environmental patterns and support data interpretation and resource management.

Challenges to implementation include equipment costs, data management, and technical capacity. Programs that provide training, financial support, and collaborative research partnerships help address these barriers. Policy support and regulatory integration help scale the use of smart fishing and monitoring technologies across marine sectors.

Smart fishing tools, observation networks, and waste monitoring systems enhance sustainability by improving transparency, enabling adaptive management, and reducing environmental impacts across marine activities.

Bio-Based Materials and Marine Bioproducts

Bio-based materials and marine bioproducts contribute to circularity in the Blue Economy by reducing dependence on fossil-based resources and supporting the sustainable use of marine biomass. These materials are derived from marine organisms such as algae, seaweed, shellfish, and microorganisms, and they offer alternatives for packaging, textiles, chemicals, and other industrial applications. The development of marine bioproducts supports innovation, enhances resource efficiency, and promotes regenerative practices that align with the protection of ocean ecosystems.

Algae and seaweed are among the most prominent sources of marine bio-based materials. They grow rapidly, require no freshwater or fertilizer, and absorb carbon dioxide as they develop. This makes them suitable for producing a range of bioproducts, including bioplastics, biofuels, cosmetics, pharmaceuticals, and dietary supplements. Seaweed-based bioplastics offer potential alternatives to conventional plastics and can be designed to biodegrade under specific conditions. Their production can help reduce marine pollution by replacing materials that persist in the environment. Large-scale seaweed cultivation also provides co-benefits such as nutrient uptake, habitat creation, and shoreline protection.

Microalgae provide additional opportunities for sustainable material development. These microorganisms can produce high-value compounds such as pigments, antioxidants, omega-3 fatty acids, and bioactive molecules. Microalgae can be cultivated in controlled environments, including bioreactors or wastewater treatment systems, enabling efficient resource use and reducing environmental impacts. Microalgal biomass serves as a feedstock for biofuels, reducing reliance on fossil fuels and contributing to decarbonization. Advances in biotechnology improve the efficiency of microalgae cultivation and expand the range of commercial applications.

Shellfish and crustaceans contribute to bio-based material production through the extraction of chitin and chitosan. These compounds, derived from shells and exoskeletons, are used in water treatment, agriculture, medicine, and packaging. Chitosan has antimicrobial properties and can be incorporated into biodegradable films and coatings. The use of shellfish byproducts helps reduce waste from seafood processing and supports circular value chains. Processing techniques continue to improve the purity and functionality of chitin-based materials, increasing their suitability for diverse industrial applications.

Marine bacteria and fungi produce enzymes, polymers, and metabolites that serve as bases for bioproduct development. These microorganisms thrive in extreme ocean environments and produce compounds with unique properties, such as heat resistance or pressure tolerance. Marine enzymes are used in pharmaceuticals, food processing, and environmental remediation. Biopolymers produced by marine microorganisms hold potential for developing biodegradable plastics and specialty chemicals. Research into marine genetic resources expands the range of possible applications for bioproducts derived from microbial processes.

Fishery and aquaculture byproducts offer another significant source of marine bioproducts. Collagen, gelatin, fish oils, and protein hydrolysates extracted from heads, skins, and bones are used in food, cosmetics, nutraceuticals, and industrial applications. These compounds add value to materials that would otherwise be discarded, supporting resource efficiency and reducing waste. Fishmeal and fish oil remain important inputs for aquaculture, and efforts to improve processing and increase yields support circularity within the seafood value chain. New extraction technologies enhance the quality and functionality of these bioproducts.

Innovation in marine bio-based materials depends on sustainable sourcing and careful management of marine ecosystems. Wild harvesting of seaweed or other biomass must be conducted in ways that maintain ecological balance and avoid habitat disruption. Cultivation practices should incorporate ecosystem considerations, ensuring that nutrient flows, water quality, and biodiversity are preserved. Integrated multi-trophic aquaculture systems support sustainable biomass production by pairing seaweed or shellfish cultivation with fish farming, allowing nutrients from fish waste to support plant growth.

Research and development are crucial for advancing bio-based materials and expanding their commercial viability. Scientists and industry partners work to improve material properties, reduce production costs, and develop scalable manufacturing processes. Innovations in biorefinery technologies enable the extraction of multiple high-value compounds from a single biomass source, improving economic viability. Efforts to develop standards and certifications help ensure that marine bioproducts meet environmental and quality requirements.

Market development supports the adoption of bio-based materials by creating demand and integrating these products into supply chains. Partnerships between material producers, manufacturers, and retailers help expand applications for marine bioproducts. Public procurement policies that favor sustainable materials can accelerate market growth. Consumer awareness also influences adoption, particularly for biodegradable packaging and eco-friendly products.

Marine bioproducts require supportive policy environments that encourage research, regulate sustainable harvesting, and facilitate investment in biomanufacturing infrastructure. Clear guidelines for environmental protection, licensing, and product safety help build investor and consumer confidence. International cooperation supports knowledge exchange and harmonizes standards for bio-based materials.

Bio-based materials and marine bioproducts provide opportunities to reduce environmental impacts, enhance circularity, and support sustainable economic development within the Blue Economy.

Challenges: Data Governance, Access, and Equity

Data governance, access, and equity present significant challenges as digital technologies become more integrated into marine resource management. Effective oversight of data is essential for ensuring that information is collected, shared, and used responsibly. As more sensors, platforms, and monitoring systems generate large volumes of data, issues related to ownership, privacy, security, and interoperability become increasingly important. Addressing these challenges helps ensure that digital tools contribute to sustainable and inclusive management of ocean resources.

Data governance frameworks determine how data is stored, accessed, and shared among stakeholders. In marine sectors, data often comes from diverse sources, including satellites, vessels, sensors, research programs, and community initiatives. Without clear governance structures, information can become fragmented or inaccessible. Data standards help ensure consistency in measurement methods, formats, and reporting practices. Interoperable systems allow different datasets to be combined, supporting more comprehensive analysis and decision-making. When governance frameworks are weak, duplication of effort or gaps in monitoring can limit the effectiveness of digital tools.

Ownership and control of data are central considerations in governance. Private companies operating vessels, aquaculture facilities, or monitoring systems may view data as proprietary, restricting access to protect commercial interests. Governments may classify certain datasets as sensitive for security or regulatory purposes. Researchers and communities may have concerns about how their data will be used, especially if it includes information about culturally significant areas or livelihood practices. Clear agreements on data rights help address these concerns by outlining responsibilities and permissible uses. Transparent governance fosters trust among users and encourages broader participation in data-sharing initiatives.

Data privacy and security are increasingly important as digital technologies proliferate. IoT sensors, vessel monitoring systems, and blockchain applications generate detailed information about locations, operations, and environmental conditions. Unauthorized access or misuse of this information can pose risks to businesses, communities, and national security. Cybersecurity measures, encryption protocols, and secure data storage are necessary to protect sensitive information. Establishing procedures for responding to data breaches helps mitigate impacts and maintain confidence in digital systems.

Access to data is another challenge, particularly for small-scale fishers, Indigenous communities, and developing countries. Many digital platforms require specialized equipment, stable internet connections, and technical skills that may not be widely available. Cost barriers can further limit access, as advanced monitoring tools and subscription-based data services may be unaffordable for smaller operators. Limited access can create inequalities in who benefits from digital innovation, reinforcing existing disparities within marine sectors. Efforts to increase accessibility through open-data initiatives, simplified technologies, and financial support help address these challenges.

Capacity building is essential for ensuring equitable access to digital tools and data. Training programs that teach users how to interpret information, operate equipment, and apply data to resource management help broaden participation. Local institutions benefit from technical support that strengthens data collection, processing, and analysis capabilities. Collaborative learning platforms and peer-to-peer exchanges help share knowledge and build confidence in using digital technologies. Capacity-building efforts should reflect local contexts and priorities to ensure that tools are useful and relevant.

Equity considerations extend to how data is used in decision-making. Communities that rely on marine resources may be affected by policies or management decisions that draw on digital data. Ensuring that these communities have a role in interpreting data and shaping governance frameworks supports more inclusive and legitimate decision-making processes. Participatory approaches, such as co-management and community-based monitoring, allow local knowledge to complement digital information and ensure that decisions reflect diverse perspectives.

Language, cultural context, and data interpretation also influence equity. Digital tools often rely on technical terminology or interfaces that may not be accessible to all users. Translating data platforms, providing visualizations, and offering support in local languages improve usability. Recognizing the value of local and Indigenous knowledge encourages more collaborative data practices that respect cultural values and strengthen resource stewardship.

Data quality and reliability are additional challenges. Inconsistent data collection methods, equipment malfunctions, and environmental variability can affect accuracy. Incomplete datasets may lead to misinterpretation or flawed decisions. Establishing protocols for equipment maintenance, calibration, and validation improves reliability. Transparent documentation of data sources and methods helps ensure that users understand limitations and uncertainties.

International cooperation supports improvements in data governance, access, and equity. Many marine issues cross national boundaries, requiring shared monitoring systems and coordinated policies. Regional data platforms, joint research programs, and harmonized standards help integrate information across countries and sectors. Cooperation strengthens collective capacity to manage marine resources sustainably.

Addressing challenges of data governance, access, and equity is essential for ensuring that digital technologies support inclusive and effective marine resource management.

Chapter 9: Circular Blue Economy for Coastal Communities and Livelihoods

This chapter assesses how circular models can support resilient and inclusive coastal communities. It explores opportunities for sustainable livelihoods, local entrepreneurship, and community-driven resource management. The chapter emphasizes the importance of capacity building, social inclusion, and climate adaptation in strengthening coastal resilience.

Community-Driven Circular Models for Local Development

Community-driven circular models for local development place coastal and Indigenous communities at the center of designing, implementing, and managing sustainable ocean-based activities. These models build on local knowledge, social structures, and environmental priorities to create systems that reduce waste, improve resource efficiency, and support resilient livelihoods. By focusing on community empowerment and localized decision-making, these approaches ensure that circular solutions reflect local needs and contribute to long-term social and environmental well-being.

Local resource stewardship is a core feature of community-driven circular models. Many coastal communities have long-standing practices for managing fisheries, harvesting seaweed, and maintaining coastal ecosystems. These practices often emphasize balance, regeneration, and shared responsibility for common resources. Community-based fisheries management, for example, allows local groups to establish harvest rules, monitor compliance, and protect critical habitats. These systems help maintain fish stocks, reduce illegal activities, and support sustainable livelihoods. They also strengthen social cohesion and collective agency.

Circularity in local development often begins with waste reduction and resource recovery at the community level. Coastal communities develop systems for separating waste, collecting recyclable materials, and repurposing organic waste for compost or energy production. Small-scale recycling centers process plastics, glass, and metals, generating income and reducing environmental impacts. Fishing communities often develop initiatives to collect and recycle used gear, ropes, and nets, helping prevent marine litter. Local enterprises may repurpose old fishing gear into crafts, textiles, or construction materials, creating new revenue streams.

Food systems provide important opportunities for community-led circularity. Coastal communities engaged in aquaculture or small-scale fisheries can adopt practices that reduce waste and improve resource efficiency. Examples include processing byproducts into fishmeal or fertilizers, using organic waste to support seaweed or shellfish production, and applying integrated multi-species systems that mimic natural food webs. Community-supported fisheries programs allow local residents to purchase seafood directly from fishers, reducing transportation emissions and reducing waste associated with long supply chains.

Nature-based solutions are often central to community-driven circular models. Communities restore mangroves, wetlands, dunes, and reef systems to protect shorelines, enhance biodiversity, and support carbon sequestration. These efforts use local labor, traditional knowledge, and community governance structures. Restored ecosystems provide co-benefits such as improved fisheries, enhanced tourism opportunities, and strengthened climate resilience. Community participation ensures that projects reflect cultural values and local priorities.

Entrepreneurship is an important component of circular local development. Community members establish small businesses that produce value-added products from local resources, such as seaweed snacks, natural cosmetics, marine bioproducts, or eco-friendly handicrafts. Training programs help local entrepreneurs develop skills in business management, marketing, and sustainable

101

production. Access to microfinance or cooperative funding supports the development of small enterprises. These initiatives diversify income sources and reduce dependence on a narrow set of economic activities.

Education and capacity building support the long-term viability of community-driven models. Workshops, training programs, and school-based initiatives raise awareness of circular practices and environmental stewardship. Skill-building programs in areas such as data collection, aquaculture management, waste sorting, and resource monitoring empower community members to lead local initiatives. Partnerships with universities, NGOs, and government agencies provide technical support, resources, and opportunities for knowledge exchange.

Community governance structures shape how circular models are implemented. Councils, cooperatives, and local associations manage resource use, coordinate activities, and facilitate decision-making. These structures ensure that community voices guide project development and that benefits are distributed equitably. Transparent governance builds trust and encourages participation. Customary governance systems, where present, help integrate cultural norms and traditional decision-making processes into modern circular initiatives.

Tourism offers opportunities for community-led circular development when managed responsibly. Eco-tourism initiatives highlight local culture, biodiversity, and conservation efforts while generating income. Community-run lodges, guided tours, and cultural experiences support local employment and reduce environmental impacts associated with conventional tourism. Circular models can include waste-free tourism practices, local sourcing of food and materials, and visitor education programs.

Partnerships with external stakeholders enhance community capacity while preserving local control. Governments can support community-led initiatives through regulatory frameworks, funding programs, and infrastructure investments. NGOs provide training, technical assistance, and resources for project implementation. Private companies may collaborate with communities through fair-trade agreements, supply chain partnerships, or procurement programs that prioritize sustainable local products.

Monitoring and evaluation strengthen community-driven circular models by providing insights into environmental, social, and economic outcomes. Community members often participate in data collection, such as tracking fish stocks, monitoring water quality, or assessing waste reduction. Local involvement in monitoring fosters ownership and ensures that evaluation methods reflect community priorities.

Community-driven circular models for local development promote sustainable resource use, empower local actors, and support resilient and diversified coastal economies.

Gender, Youth, and Social Inclusion

Gender, youth, and social inclusion are critical elements of circular blue economy transitions, ensuring that the benefits of sustainable ocean development are equitably shared across society. Addressing inclusion strengthens community resilience, broadens participation in marine sectors, and supports more diverse knowledge systems. Inclusive approaches recognize the unique contributions, needs, and experiences of groups that have historically faced barriers in accessing opportunities in fisheries, aquaculture, coastal tourism, and marine conservation.

Gender considerations are essential because women play significant roles in many coastal and marine value chains. Women often participate in fish processing, seaweed farming, shellfish harvesting, marketing, and small-scale aquaculture, yet their contributions are frequently undervalued and underrepresented in decision-making. Barriers such as limited access to finance, restricted land rights, and unequal participation in leadership positions limit their ability to influence policies and benefit fully from circular initiatives. Supporting gender inclusion involves improving access to training, technology, and financial resources. Policies that formalize women's roles, strengthen labor protections, and promote equitable representation in marine governance help ensure that circular models reflect the perspectives and priorities of women in coastal communities.

Youth play an important role in advancing innovation and sustainability within the circular blue economy. Young people often adopt digital tools quickly and bring new ideas to areas such as aquaculture automation, ocean monitoring, and waste reduction. However, youth face challenges including limited employment opportunities, skills gaps, and migration pressures in many coastal regions. Education and workforce development programs help equip young people with technical, entrepreneurial, and digital skills relevant to emerging sectors. Youth-led enterprises and innovation hubs foster new business models that integrate circular principles. Inclusive policies that support youth engagement in marine governance encourage long-term stewardship and help communities adapt to changing economic conditions.

Social inclusion encompasses a broader set of considerations, ensuring that marginalized or vulnerable groups have access to the opportunities created by circular blue economy development. These groups may include small-scale fishers, Indigenous communities, migrants, people with disabilities, and low-income households. Socially inclusive approaches recognize that communities are diverse and that people experience environmental and economic changes differently. Efforts to expand access to sustainable livelihoods, build adaptive capacity, and reduce vulnerability contribute to more stable and resilient coastal societies.

Indigenous communities bring extensive ecological knowledge and culturally grounded management practices that align closely with circular principles. Their understanding of seasonal cycles, species behavior, and ecosystem interactions supports sustainable resource use. Respecting Indigenous rights, supporting self-determination, and integrating traditional knowledge into marine planning enhance both environmental outcomes and cultural integrity. Co-management arrangements and legal recognition of customary marine tenure help create equitable governance systems.

Inclusion also involves addressing the structural barriers that prevent certain groups from participating fully in marine activities. These barriers may arise from unequal access to education, limited mobility, discriminatory practices, or insufficient infrastructure. Programs that expand access to credit, provide affordable technology, or improve transportation and communication networks help reduce disparities. Social safety nets and community support systems can buffer vulnerable groups from economic shocks, particularly in regions dependent on climate-sensitive sectors.

Access to digital tools and information is another dimension of inclusion. Digital platforms are becoming increasingly important for monitoring resources, managing supply chains, and accessing markets. Ensuring that women, youth, and marginalized communities can use these tools helps avoid widening inequalities. Training programs, affordable connectivity, and user-friendly interfaces support broader participation. Collaborative digital initiatives that incorporate local languages and cultural contexts improve accessibility and relevance.

Inclusive governance strengthens community participation and ensures that diverse voices influence policy and management decisions. Creating spaces for dialogue, consultation, and shared decision-making helps account for different needs and priorities. Representation of women, youth, and marginalized groups in councils, cooperatives, and advisory boards promotes more balanced and equitable outcomes. Transparent processes help build trust and encourage continued engagement.

Monitoring and evaluation of inclusion outcomes support the development of more equitable circular blue economy initiatives. Disaggregated data on participation, income, resource access, and training can reveal gaps and guide targeted interventions. Community-based monitoring programs allow people from diverse groups to contribute to data collection and interpretation, strengthening ownership and accountability.

Addressing gender, youth, and social inclusion supports more resilient and adaptable coastal communities by ensuring that circular blue economy transitions are shaped by a wide range of perspectives and that benefits extend across society.

Capacity Building, Education, and Local Entrepreneurship

Capacity building, education, and local entrepreneurship are central to advancing circular practices within coastal and marine economies. These elements strengthen human capital, enhance local ownership of resources, and create pathways for communities to participate in sustainable economic development. By equipping individuals and institutions with the knowledge and skills needed to adopt and maintain circular systems, capacity building reinforces long-term resilience and supports inclusive transitions toward regenerative ocean economies.

Capacity building focuses on developing the technical, managerial, and institutional abilities required to implement and sustain circular initiatives. Training programs improve understanding of marine resource management, waste reduction, aquaculture practices, and ecosystem restoration. Workshops and hands-on demonstrations help community members apply new techniques to local contexts, such as improved fish processing methods, seaweed cultivation, or selective fishing gear. Institutional capacity is strengthened through support for local cooperatives, community associations, and governance bodies that oversee resource use. Strengthening administrative and organizational capacity helps ensure that communities can manage projects, coordinate stakeholders, and comply with regulatory requirements.

Education expands opportunities for individuals within coastal communities to develop knowledge that supports sustainable livelihoods. School curricula that incorporate marine conservation, circular economy principles, and environmental stewardship encourage early engagement in sustainable practices. Higher education programs in marine science, environmental technology, and coastal engineering provide opportunities for youth to pursue careers in emerging blue economy sectors. Technical and vocational training equips workers with practical skills such as aquaculture operations, boat maintenance, waste management, and digital literacy. Partnerships between schools, universities, and community organizations help integrate local knowledge and ensure that educational programs address community-specific needs.

Knowledge exchange is an important dimension of education and capacity building. Peer-to-peer learning initiatives allow fishers, farmers, and small business owners to share experiences, tools, and techniques. Exchange visits between communities expose participants to different circular practices, such as community recycling systems, resource recovery methods, or integrated aquaculture models. Collaboration with research institutions and NGOs provides access to scientific insights, technical expertise, and supportive networks that help communities refine and expand their initiatives.

Local entrepreneurship plays a significant role in translating circular economy principles into practical economic activities. Entrepreneurs develop value-added products, services, and business models that reduce waste, improve resource efficiency, or create new markets for sustainable materials. In coastal communities, entrepreneurship opportunities may include processing seafood byproducts into bioproducts, producing seaweed-based foods, developing eco-friendly packaging, offering eco-tourism services, or creating gear-recycling enterprises. These ventures support livelihood diversification and reduce dependence on vulnerable or declining resources.

Access to finance is essential for fostering local entrepreneurship. Microfinance programs, cooperative savings groups, and community investment schemes help entrepreneurs acquire the capital needed to purchase equipment, expand production, or adopt new technologies. Governments and development organizations can support entrepreneurship by offering grants, low-interest loans, or subsidies for sustainable technologies. Financial literacy programs enable entrepreneurs to manage budgets, plan investments, and assess business risks. Inclusive finance initiatives ensure that women, youth, and marginalized groups can access financial resources.

Innovation hubs and incubators provide infrastructure and support for local entrepreneurs. These centers offer workspace, mentoring, technical assistance, and networking opportunities. They create environments where new ideas can be tested, refined, and scaled. Partnerships between innovation hubs, universities, and private companies contribute to knowledge transfer and help entrepreneurs adopt advanced technologies such as digital monitoring systems or bio-based material production. Local incubators grounded in community needs ensure that innovation aligns with cultural, environmental, and economic priorities.

Policy support strengthens capacity building and entrepreneurship by creating enabling environments for sustainable development. National and regional policies that prioritize vocational training, educational investment, and small business support can accelerate circular transitions. Regulations that encourage waste reduction, sustainable harvesting, and environmental protection create incentives for circular business models. Public procurement policies may favor environmentally responsible products or services, creating new market opportunities for local enterprises.

Community involvement enhances the effectiveness of capacity-building and entrepreneurship initiatives. Local leaders, cooperatives, and community associations help identify training needs, select appropriate technologies, and coordinate development activities. Inclusive participation ensures that programs benefit a wide range of individuals and address gaps in access or representation. Community-driven initiatives also draw on traditional knowledge and cultural practices, integrating them with new skills and technologies.

Monitoring and evaluation contribute to continuous improvement of capacity-building and entrepreneurial programs. Tracking participation, skill development, business outcomes, and environmental impacts helps identify successful approaches and areas for refinement. Community-based monitoring allows local participants to evaluate their progress and adjust strategies as needed. Sharing results across communities and institutions supports broader learning and strengthens regional networks.

Capacity building, education, and local entrepreneurship work together to empower coastal communities, enhance resource management, and support sustainable economic development within circular blue economy frameworks.

Climate Adaptation and Resilience in Coastal Zones

Climate adaptation and resilience in coastal zones are essential components of circular blue economy strategies, as coastal regions face increasing risks from sea-level rise, extreme weather events, erosion, saltwater intrusion, and ecosystem degradation. Strengthening resilience requires approaches that reduce vulnerability, enhance ecosystem health, and support sustainable livelihoods. Adaptation measures must integrate environmental, social, and economic considerations to ensure that communities and ecosystems can adjust to changing conditions over time.

Ecosystem-based adaptation is a central approach to enhancing resilience in coastal zones. Restoring and protecting natural systems such as mangroves, salt marshes, coral reefs, dunes, and seagrass meadows improves the capacity of coastlines to absorb wave energy, store carbon, and maintain biodiversity. These ecosystems contribute to shoreline stabilization, reduce the impacts of storms, and support fisheries and other marine livelihoods. Their restoration often relies on community engagement, local labor, and traditional knowledge, reinforcing linkages between ecological health and social well-being. Integrating nature-based solutions into coastal planning reduces dependence on hard infrastructure and supports long-term environmental stability.

Coastal infrastructure must be designed or retrofitted to withstand the impacts of climate change. Resilient infrastructure includes elevated buildings, flood-resistant designs, permeable surfaces, green roofs, and protective barriers integrated with natural features. Ports, roads, and wastewater systems require adaptation to manage increased precipitation, storm surges, and operational disruptions. Incorporating circular design principles, such as modular components and recyclable materials, supports resilience by making infrastructure easier to repair, upgrade, or repurpose. Strategic planning ensures that coastal development avoids high-risk areas and prioritizes long-term safety.

Community preparedness is another critical component of coastal resilience. Early-warning systems for storms, floods, and coastal hazards improve safety and reduce losses. Training programs help residents understand risks, develop emergency plans, and respond effectively to disasters. Community-based monitoring of shoreline changes, water quality, and ecosystem health provides valuable information for adaptive management. Inclusive preparedness efforts ensure that vulnerable groups, including women, youth, the elderly, and low-income households, have access to resources and support during extreme events.

Water resource management plays an important role in adapting to climate-driven changes in coastal zones. Sea-level rise and saltwater intrusion can compromise freshwater supplies, affecting drinking water, agriculture, and industry. Integrated water management strategies, such as rainwater harvesting, aquifer recharge, efficient irrigation, and water recycling, help maintain water security. Coastal wetlands and mangrove systems support water filtration and reduce contamination risks. Planning decisions must consider future climate scenarios to ensure that water systems remain reliable under changing conditions.

Climate-resilient livelihoods strengthen community stability and reduce dependence on vulnerable economic sectors. Diversifying income sources through sustainable aquaculture, eco-tourism, value-added processing, or marine bioproduct development can reduce pressure on declining fisheries and provide alternatives during environmental shocks. Training and financial support enable community members to adopt new livelihood strategies that align with local skills and environmental conditions. Empowering women and youth to participate in climate-resilient economic activities broadens the range of community capacities and strengthens adaptive potential.

Governance plays a crucial role in supporting climate adaptation and resilience. Integrated coastal zone management frameworks coordinate actions across sectors such as fisheries, tourism, biodiversity conservation, and urban development. Policies that incorporate climate risk assessments, enforce land-use regulations, and guide infrastructure development support proactive adaptation. Local governance structures, including community councils and cooperatives, help reflect local priorities and knowledge in planning decisions. Collaborative governance ensures that adaptation measures align with cultural values and local development objectives.

Finance mechanisms support the implementation of adaptation measures in coastal zones. Government budgets, climate funds, insurance schemes, and blended finance models can provide resources for ecosystem restoration, resilient infrastructure, and community training programs. Microfinance and cooperative funding help households and small businesses adopt adaptation technologies or diversify livelihoods. Economic instruments such as carbon credits, payment for ecosystem services, and resilience bonds create incentives for restoration and risk reduction.

Research and data play a foundational role in guiding adaptation strategies. Climate models, hazard maps, and environmental monitoring systems provide insights into future risks and ecosystem responses. Collaboration between researchers, community members, and policymakers ensures that adaptation actions reflect both scientific knowledge and local experience. Continuous monitoring allows adaptation strategies to evolve as conditions change.

Climate adaptation and resilience in coastal zones require integrated approaches that strengthen ecosystems, support communities, and guide sustainable development.

Conclusion

The circular blue economy offers a pathway for managing ocean resources in a way that supports environmental regeneration, economic opportunity, and social well-being. It shifts attention from extractive and linear models toward systems that value resource efficiency, ecosystem health, and long-term sustainability. This approach requires collaboration across governments, industries, financial institutions, scientific communities, and coastal populations to create integrated solutions that reflect both global priorities and local realities.

Strengthening governance is an essential foundation for advancing circularity. Policy frameworks that incorporate ecosystem protection, sustainable resource use, and equitable access guide the transformation of marine sectors. International agreements, national ocean strategies, and regional cooperation mechanisms help align actions across jurisdictions. Effective governance also depends on transparent decision-making, robust regulatory systems, and recognition of the rights and roles of coastal and Indigenous communities. These elements provide stability for investment and support environmental safeguards.

Innovation and finance play important roles in scaling circular models. Technological developments such as digital monitoring systems, AI-driven tools, and bio-based materials help improve efficiency, transparency, and environmental outcomes. Financial mechanisms, including blue bonds, blended finance, and impact investment, support the development of new infrastructure, sustainable enterprises, and restoration projects. Integrating environmental and social criteria into investment decisions ensures that financial flows contribute to long-term resilience rather than short-term extraction.

Healthy ecosystems underpin the success of circular blue economies. Restoring and protecting marine habitats enhances biodiversity, strengthens climate resilience, and supports livelihoods dependent on fisheries, aquaculture, and coastal tourism. Nature-based solutions, such as mangrove restoration and coral rehabilitation, complement engineered systems and help reduce the impacts of climate change. Effective management of marine pollution, waste systems, and resource extraction contributes to the regeneration of ecosystems.

Communities are central actors in circular transitions. Local knowledge, cultural practices, and community-driven initiatives help shape approaches that are context-specific and socially grounded. Opportunities for sustainable livelihoods, skills development, and entrepreneurship ensure that circular models contribute to inclusive development. Support for women, youth, and marginalized groups strengthens social cohesion and broadens participation in emerging blue economy sectors.

Data and digital systems support informed decision-making. Reliable information on environmental conditions, resource use, and economic activities helps guide adaptive management and improve accountability. Data governance frameworks ensure that information is managed responsibly, with attention to privacy, access, and equity. Investments in digital capacity enable communities and institutions to benefit from technological advancements and participate actively in resource management.

The transition to a circular blue economy involves long-term planning, continuous learning, and flexible approaches that can respond to changing environmental and socio-economic conditions. Collaboration across disciplines and sectors helps create integrated solutions that address complex ocean challenges. By focusing on regeneration, efficiency, and inclusion, the circular blue economy provides a framework for sustaining marine ecosystems while supporting communities and industries that depend on them.

The adoption of circular principles in ocean-related sectors can contribute to resilient economies, healthier ecosystems, and more equitable societies. As countries and communities work to address climate change, biodiversity loss, and resource pressures, the circular blue economy offers a direction for aligning environmental protection with sustainable development.

www.ingramcontent.com/pod-product-compliance
Lightning Source LLC
Chambersburg PA
CBHW060270270226

41930CB00012B/2946